25<u>00</u>

The GUINNESS Book of Autographs

To the King's most excellent Majesty
in Council.

The Petition of Benjamin Franklin, LLD.

Most humbly sheweth

That your Petitioner being desirous of under-
taking the Settlement of a Tract of Land in your Majesty's
newly established Province of Nova Scotia, in America,
humbly prays, that your Majesty will be graciously
pleased to give Orders to your Majesty's Governor, to pass
a Patent to your Petitioner of Twenty Thousand Acres
of Land in such Parts of the said Province as your Petitioner or his Agent shall chuse, upon the same Terms
and Conditions on which Lands have been granted to other
your Majesty's Subjects within the said Province.

And the Petitioner, as in Duty bound
shall ever pray, &c

B Franklin

The GUINNESS Book of Autographs

Ray Rawlins

Guinness Superlatives Ltd
2 Cecil Court, London Road, Enfield, Middlesex

First published 1977

Copyright © 1977 Ray Rawlins and Guinness Superlatives Ltd

Published in Great Britain by
Guinness Superlatives Ltd,
2 Cecil Court, London Road, Enfield,
Middlesex

ISBN 0 900424 73 7

'Guinness' is a registered trade mark of Arthur Guinness Son & Company Ltd

By the same author *Four Hundred Years of British Autographs*

Set in 'Monophoto' Baskerville Series 169
Printed and bound in Great Britain by
Jarrold & Sons Ltd, Norwich

For Sue

Frontispiece Franklin writes to George III. An entirely holograph petition from *Benjamin Franklin*, American statesman, scientist and philosopher to **King George III** for the grant to him of 20,000 acres of land in Nova Scotia. Signed 'B. Franklin', February 1766. (Public Record Office, London.)

ACKNOWLEDGEMENTS

The author gratefully acknowledges the following for advice on, and for the provision of, material:

Ronnie Aldrich, Esq.; Algemeen Rijksarchief, 's Gravenhage, Holland (J Fox, Deputy Keeper, Third Archives); Eric Allen, Esq.; Archives Nationales, Paris (R Marquant, Conservateur-en-Chef); Argentine Embassy, London (Counsellor G Figari); Miss Ruth Bailey; Mr Conway Barker, La Marque, Texas, USA; Basel University, Switzerland (Öffentliche Bibliotek); Signora Elena Battachi Brini; Belgian Embassy, London; Benezit; Bibliotèque Nationale, Paris; Mr Julius Bisno, Los Angeles, USA; Prof. P Boyde, Faculty of Modern and Medieval Languages, Cambridge University; The British (Museum) Library (Mr T S Pattie); Gerald Burdon, Esq., Sotheby's, London; Canadian High Commission, London (Library, Mrs S Yates; Cultural Section Mrs Garneau); Cape Archives, Capetown, South Africa (Miss Joan Davis, Chief Archivist); Msr Michel Castaing, Maison Charavay, Paris; Chinese (P.R.) Embassy, London; The Library of Congress, Washington, D.C. USA; P J Croft, Esq., Librarian, King's College, Cambridge; Daimler Benz Aktiengessellshaft Archiv-Geschichte (Museum) (Dr Huegel); Royal Danish Embassy, London (Minister, Press and Cultural Affairs, Mr Henry Agerbak); Danish Ministry of Foreign Affairs, Copenhagen; Richard Davis, Esq.; Dr V A Depasquale, Librarian Royal Malta Library; Mrs Joan Duggan; Egyptian Embassy (Arab Republic of Egypt), London (Fawzi Abdel Zaher, Cultural Counsellor); Paul Emezy; Mrs Joan Enders, Albuquerque, New Mexico, USA; Finnish Embassy, London; Embassy of France, London (Msr Jean-Loup Bourget, Cultural Attache); French Institute, South Kensington, London; Miss Beatrice Frei; Mr Joseph J Fricelli, New York, USA; C H Geigy, Autographen; German Institute, London (Fr. Niemoller, Librarian); Alan Gill, Esq.; W Godward, Esq.; Greek Embassy, London (C Verros, Information Officer); Greek Ministry of Culture and Science, Athens; G H Green, Esq., Librarian, Hispanic and Luso Brazilian Council, Canning House, London; Haarlem-Archief Der Gemeente, Holland (Dr F Tames, Archivist); Mr Charles Hamilton, New York, USA; Sonia Henie-Niels Opstad Foundations, Høvikodden, Norway; Peter Hildreth, Esq.; Mr and Mrs Dane Human; Miss K Hunt; Dr J Ibáñez Cerda, Director, Biblioteca, Instituto de Cultura Hispanica, Madrid; Imperial War Museum, London; Indonesian Embassy, London; Isle of Man Government Reprographic Dept (R Shimmin, Esq.); Italian Institute, London (Prof. M Tassoni, Dr Nino Spallone; Japanese Embassy, London (Mrs Conte-Holm, Information Officer); Theo Johnson, Esq.; Keigs Photographers, Douglas, Isle of Man; Kent County Archives; Korean Embassy, London; Mr Ernst Krenek; Mr Neale Lanigan, Jnr, Fairview Village, USA; Biblioteca Laurenziana, Florence (Professoressa Manzini); Peter Lawrence, Esq.; Linnean Society of London; The London Library; Mr M H Loewenstern, Amarillo, Texas, USA; Norris McWhirter, Esq.; Maggs Bros., London (Miss Hinda Rose); Mr Frank Martin; Sir Brian Marwick; Mr Klaus Mecklenburg, Stargardt, Marburg, Germany; Mexican Embassy, London (Counsellor H. Flores-Sanchez); Mrs T G Moore; Musée de L'Aire, Paris; Mr and Mrs Vladimir Nabokov; National Gallery, London (Mrs C Robinson, Librarian); Norwegian Embassy, London; Peter Owen, Ltd; The Pakistan Embassy, London; Mr Adrian Peñalver Parejo; The Polish Library, London (Dr Z Jogodzinsky); The Portuguese Embassy, London; Public Record Office, London (Mr E K Timings, Mr N A M Rodger, Mr C J Edwards); Prof. D B Quinn, Dept of Medieval History, Liverpool University; J C Quinton, Esq., Chief Librarian, South African Parliament; Diana J Rendell and Kenneth W Rendell, Newton, Mass., USA; Richmond Borough Council (Library); Rijksmuseum Voor de Geschiedenis der Natuurwetenschappen,

Leyden, Holland (Dr G A C Veeneman); Pastor J F Rowlands; Msr Renato Saggiori, Apt, France; The Science Museum, London (Dr A B Thomas, Mr Brian Lee); The National Library of Scotland (Dr T I Rae, Keeper of Mss); South African Embassy, London; Spanish Embassy, London (Mr Luis Villaba, Information Minister, Mr José M Alonso Gama, Cultural Affairs Minister, Miss Diana Blackwell); Spanish Institute, London (Mr Vega Escandon, Librarian); Royal Swedish Embassy, London (Mr Pia Sparrström, Scientific Section); Royal Swedish Library, Stockholm; Sir Michael Tippett; Turkish Archives General Directorate; Turkish Ministry of Culture, Ankara; Madame Tussaud's, London; Embassy of the USA, London (Dr Charles R Ritcheson, Cultural Attache); Donald Weeks, Esq.; Miss Doreen Wells; John Wilson, Esq., Isle of Man; John Wilson, Esq., Witney, Oxon.; Prof. J H Whitfield, Dept of Italian, Birmingham University; Zentralbibliothek, Zurich, Switzerland.

SPECIAL ACKNOWLEDGEMENTS

A number of individuals and institutions whose co-operation has been considerable, are due my specific thanks for their invaluable help.

This has been forthcoming from two distinguished American collectors, Mr Julius Bisno of Los Angeles and Mr M. H. Loewenstern of Amarillo, Texas and the Isle of Man collector, Mr Richard Davis. The prominent Continental autograph dealers Msr Michel Castaing of Charavay, Paris, Herr Klaus Mecklenburg of Stargardt, Marburg, Germany and Msr Renato Saggiori of Meylan, France have permitted me extensive usage of their catalogues and have also given me much expert advice. Leading United States dealers Mr Conway Barker of La Marque, Texas, Mr Joseph J Fricelli of New York and Mr Neale Lanigan, Jnr of Fairview Village, Pennsylvania have provided much useful material.

Autograph authority and author Mr Charles Hamilton of New York has kindly allowed me use of a number of facsimiles from his works, in particular from his *Collecting Autographs and Manuscripts* (University of Oklahoma Press, 1961), whilst British Olympic athlete and writer, Mr Peter Hildreth has permitted similar use of his book, *Name Dropper* (McWhirter, London, 1970).

Much material was also provided by the Library of Congress, Washington, the Public Record Office, London, the British (Museum) Library, London and the Biblioteca, Instituto de Cultura Hispanica, Madrid. As regards the two last-named institutions, I offer my specific thanks for their valuable help to Mr T S Pattie, Assistant Keeper of Manuscripts and to Señor Don Ibáñez Cerda, Director, respectively.

My specific thanks are also due to Mr Gerald Burdon of Sotheby's, London, Mr Adrian Penalver Parejo of Madrid; and for much excellent photographic work on the reproduction of items from my own collection, to Messrs S R Keig of Douglas, Isle of Man.

GLOSSARY OF DESCRIPTIVE ABBREVIATIONS

ADS	Autograph Document signed		LS	Letter signed
ALS	Autograph Letter signed		Ms	Manuscript
ANS	Autograph Note signed		PS [SP]	Portrait (photograph or otherwise) signed
AQS	Autograph Quotation signed			
AMsS	Autograph Manuscript signed		MsS	Manuscript signed
DS	Document signed		TLS	Typed letter signed

Preface

The main purpose of producing a work of this nature is that books containing facsimiles are necessary for collectors, librarians, Keepers of Manuscripts, students, archivists, dealers and all those who in any way handle autographs because these afford them the opportunity to identify original material by comparison with the facsimiles provided. In this book I have tried to cover a very wide spectrum and to cater for a considerable variety of tastes without losing sight of this primary aim.

The book contains facsimile autographs in many forms from plain signatures to partial or complete letters and manuscripts, signed documents and signed portraits. It spans over 1200 years of history and contains material of more than 1600 famous (and infamous) persons of all walks of life. It is international in flavour involving the great of over 70 nations past and present.

Considering the long history of autograph collecting, surprisingly few books containing any considerable number of autograph facsimiles have been published and the great majority of these have long been out of print. This book seeks to fill this gap in the facilities available for autographers, but at the same time I have attempted to make it more interesting to the younger autograph enthusiasts and to the public in general. Several departures have, therefore, been made from the usual forms of facsimile albums. Firstly, the book has been set out in an encyclopaedic alphabetical form thus saving the reader's time by eliminating the need for an index. This has not been done before. Previous books of this nature have either followed the order of professions, e.g. literature, royalty, politics, etc. or no order at all. Netherclift and Sims in *Handbook to Autographs* did follow an alphabetical grouping but did not employ anything like a strict alphabetical order. Sadly that excellent book is in any case over 100 years old and thus hopelessly outdated.

To cater for a wider public this book has been brought right up to date and many living persons have been included; and as a major difference to previous books, I have included many great names from the world of sport and entertainment which were hardly touched upon in any earlier books of this kind. Portrait illustrations were either minimal or non-existent in most other facsimile books whereas this book will include a number of portraits, several of them signed.

Whilst I have sought to include as many very famous persons as is possible in one volume, it will be appreciated that many have had to be left out. There is an immense amount of source material available and if it had been possible to use it all this book would have run into many volumes. Such a work might be of great value to specialists in autography but would not have been practicable for general publication. There are also a few cases where no autograph exists. For example, neither the great Italian poet Dante nor the famed German printer Gutenberg appear to have left behind so much as a single holograph word still remaining today. I have sought to give space to a good number of unusual names and to autographic rarities some of which are not necessarily strictly famous. Button Gwinnett the autographically exceptionally rare signer of the American Declaration of Independence comes into this latter category whilst Guy Fawkes, Mata Hari, Casanova, Houdini, 'General' Tom Thumb and Blondin can clearly be classified as unusual. Saints (literally) and sinners are equally included. St Joan of Arc and St Francis of Assisi are prominent amongst the former, 'Bluebeard' (Rais) and Crippen amongst the last-mentioned.

Certain complete groupings of 'collected' autographs will be found throughout the book. These include all the American Presidents, all the British Prime Ministers, all the Marshals of Napoleon and all British Sovereigns from Richard II onwards. There is also a page for dictionary names and another of pigs drawn blindfold with the signatures of their perpetrators!

All the items in this book are taken either from originals or from other facsimile sources. Sources are not mentioned under each entry but are listed separately and are acknowledged under major items. Here mention must be made of the existence of autopen signatures achieved with a machine, and secretarial signatures written by secretaries permitted to copy the style of their employers. Very few will be found in this book and where possible these will be identified with the necessary comment. In a few cases, however, it is virtually impossible to assert that a disputed signature is not original and even experts are not always in agreement over these. If any such examples have found their way into this book without comment, readers will still be able to use them for comparison with original material – but it is right that this warning should be sounded. Autopen signatures are used mostly in the USA whilst secretarial signatures are also used more in America than elsewhere. Surprisingly perhaps, certain of the Sovereigns of France permitted their senior personal secretaries, known as Secretaires de la Main, to sign in the same manner as themselves.

A number of autographs have had to be reduced (and a few enlarged) for space or legibility purposes, but, as people's handwriting often varies in size, this has not been indicated unless autographically necessary. In a few cases the autographs have had to be slightly 'touched up' in order to reproduce strongly but as this too has been kept to a minimum, occasional muzziness is unavoidable. Larger documents or complete letters have, of necessity, had to be reduced in many cases.

In the case of pseudonyms and titles, the persons concerned have been entered under the names by which they are more commonly known. For example, S L CLEMENS appears under 'Mark TWAIN', but Charlotte BRONTË is listed under her own name rather than her lesser known pseudonym 'Currer BELL'. Similarly, we have DISRAELI rather than BEACONSFIELD and SOULT rather than the Duke of DALMATIA. Saints will be found under their Christian names, thus THOMAS AQUINAS and IGNATIUS LOYOLA.

The correct spelling of certain names is always a problem especially where even the best of biographical dictionaries differ the one from the other. I have tried, therefore, to keep to the way in which the writer himself signed his name irrespective of whether that is or is not the accepted form today. For example, Waslav, not Vaslav, Nijinsky, De La Fontaine and Tschaikovsky. Prokofieff is a particularly good example. Every signature I have seen of his spells it with two 'f's at the end, yet in several leading works on musical biography it is spelled as culminating with one 'f' or a 'v'. I have stuck to the composer's own way of writing it. But I too have been forced to make exceptions. For instance, Cardinal Wolsey has been spelled the conventional way whereas he wrote it Wulcy. If I had listed it under the Cardinal's own spelling, the reader would have been in difficulty to find it.

Finally, as the book is essentially about autographs I have made extensive autographic comments throughout which it is hoped will assist the reader in the identification and assessment of his autographs. I have shown alternative styles of writing where appropriate and dealt at some length with controversial matters, such as the Shakespeare signatures and his disputed 'manuscript'. I have also gone into explanations of certain monarchichal *signums* such as that of Charlemagne, 'hidden' signatures like that of Sir Francis Bacon and involved signatures such as inscribed by Christopher Columbus. Scarcity and rarity when referred to imply the appearance of the material concerned on the open market not on its incidence in public institutions such as museums and national libraries, unless this is made apparent.

I hope, then, that this book will be of very real use to the serious and studious autographer as well as stimulate the interest of the less sophisticated collector; and perhaps reach out further to entertain the layman sufficiently at least for him to be able to appreciate the many-sided character of autographs, and, therefore, why we collectors collect.

Ballakilpheric   RR
Isle of Man, 1977

A Brief Introduction to Autograph Collecting

You are a nuisance

Devonshire.

Forty-five years ago, when as a schoolboy, I asked the 9th Duke of Devonshire for his autograph, he wrote the sentiment above but did not sign it until I specifically asked him to do so.

His actions taught me two things; firstly, the correct definition of an autograph and secondly, to realise how much wider could be the field of autograph collecting than simply getting together a number of signatures.

Though very many people think they are, an autograph and a signature are not synonymous. The word 'autograph' is made up of two Greek words 'auto' and 'graphos' and means 'self-writing'. Anything written by oneself is an autograph be it a single word or many thousands and it does not have to be signed. Therefore, though a signature is certainly a form of autograph, a collector of signatures would be wise to specify exactly what he requires when he approaches his 'prey'.

To the major collector of autograph material a signature by itself, though desirable if the signer is autographically very important or rare, holds far less interest than does a complete letter, an autograph manuscript, signed document, signed portrait or, in the case of a musician, some autograph music. To such collectors, which include institutions such as museums, archives, libraries and universities the world over, one of the most important ingredients of an interesting autograph is the content thereof. For example, it is far more satisfactory to have a letter concerning their work on radium by Marie or Pierre Curie, than it would be to have one by either of these great scientists simply acknowledging receipt of a formal communication. The length of a letter, especially if entirely in the handwriting of the writer – i.e. an autograph (or holograph) letter – is important but here again a short note on a vital subject will be far more pleasing and valuable than a letter rambling on for several pages on a mundane one, such as the changeable weather.

Collectors should, therefore, always aim at items which are engaging in themselves in addition to their autographic qualities, but the collecting of autographs has become so much more popular over the last decade that the type of these to be collected may well have to depend on the depth of one's purse. It is a sad fact that autographs have now become tempting to investors who are seeking an hedge against inflation in addition or as an alternative to the uncertain stock markets of today's uncertain world. Until comparatively recently, paintings, stamps and coins were much more sought after than autographs. Indeed, little was known about the latter. But of late there are more and more collectors and in consequence, more and more dealers. I will not dwell on the pros and cons of this situation which is undoubtedly here to stay. Suffice it to say that, whilst unquestionably autographs are a wise financial investment, one can but hope that the great majority of people who seek them today are doing so because of a genuine interest in history, literature or for some other aesthetic reason.

Having seen that content is of major importance, what other features will make an autograph more desirable and, frankly, more valuable? Length has been mentioned and certainly a long autograph letter on a significant subject is better than a short one. The condition of a letter can add or detract from its value especially if any of the contents have become unreadable through staining or tearing. The date – if a momentous one historically or one vital in the life of the writer – can be a factor in determining desirability. So can the addressee. A letter from Nelson to Lady Hamilton, given that the content does not affect the value, will certainly be more sought after than a letter from Nelson to someone of no interest.

As a general rule an autograph or holograph letter is more to be desired than one in the handwriting of another and only signed by the notable person concerned. In this century, with the advent of the typewriter, autograph letters are less and less common and one may well have to make do with a TLS (typed letter signed). Nonetheless, the collector can console himself that even a TLS can be of greater value than an ALS (autograph letter signed) if the content is more weighty.

Autograph values are tied up with rarity and desirability. If an autograph is not generally sought after it will not have value. Similarly, because of supply and demand, a rare autograph which is also a sought-after autograph – this is not always the same thing – will be valuable and expensive. What makes an autograph rare? One reason is when fame comes after death; another is the early death of the person concerned so that few letters survive; a third depends on the habits of the writer. Some people write very few letters, others like Wellington are prolific in their letter writing. Wellington, incidentally, lived a very long life and his fame existed for many years before his death, so that his letters are far from rare. Even so, collectors must beware of Wellington letters (except the earlier ones) as he employed a secretary who wrote in an almost identical hand, though possibly a little more legibly, to that of the Iron Duke himself.

Fame came to Shelley and Wolfe of Quebec after death and their autographs are rare. Keats, Toulouse-Lautrec, Mozart and Rupert Brooke are amongst the hundreds of famous people who died young, and their autographs too are scarce. As an outstanding contemporary example, Yuri Gagarin achieved fame as the first man in space at the age of 26 and was killed only seven years later. His early death and the fact that Russian autographs are not easily obtained, coupled with the certainty of his place in history, will make his scarce autograph a valuable rarity in the not-too-distant future.

Autographs can be subject to fashions. The Victorians were eager collectors of the letters and signatures of men of the Church – bishops and preachers. They also admired the builders of Empire. Nowadays there is little demand for autographs from these vocations. The most interest today is evinced in the letters and manuscripts of the literary great; and those of classical music and science are not far behind. Whilst the major collectors, wrongly in my opinion, show very little interest in the autographs of the worlds of sport and entertainment, these will always have their devotees.

Historical autographs are coming into their own again now as they were many years ago and I would add myself to the list of those collectors who find this the most rewarding group of all. I cannot fail to get a thrill out of the personal connection with the people who make history, good or bad. I have a long holograph draft of a speech by Charles II apologising for his behaviour towards the Scottish Covenanters whose assistance he needed to regain his throne: and when I look at this document, I think of the painful loss of his pride it must have caused this haughty young prince, still only 20, whose father had been executed by his own people only one year before. Historical autographs can tell many a tale, some, if unpublished, quite unknown to historians.

This brings me to what to collect. The main question is whether to specialise or to collect in general. A few years back I would have advocated a general collection covering all walks of life, all periods of history and all nationalities. Such a collection is my own, but then I had the advantage of starting a long time ago. Nowadays, because of the greatly increased competition, I would suggest specialising. Try collecting just the autographs of one period of history and of one profession or of one country; and even cut it down to a combination of all three of these aspects – e.g. the collecting of writers (or politicians or scientists) of the 19th century and of your own country only. Some people collect the Presidents of the USA or Popes or British (or Foreign) Prime Ministers or the Marshals and family of Napoleon. These are popular groups and will become more and more difficult to complete; and it is in any case impossible to get together a complete papal collection. Because of this, I would suggest that the would-be collector should make some other selection to accord with his own interests.

Good autograph material, now so much more in demand, is no longer easy to find. Living people can be written to or approached personally but the autographs of those no longer with us are not so readily available. There are, however, a considerable number of dealers in many countries and it is perhaps wisest, if one seeks to build up a strong collection of bygone autographs, to let one or two of these people know what one is seeking. A 'wants' list placed with a dealer is, therefore, advisable. There is also the auction market but there is no doubt that prices can get out of hand at certain auctions because of the excitement which may lead people to bid more than they intended. However, a lot of first-class material is still appearing at British, American and Continental auctions which one is unlikely to find for oneself or even in stock at a dealer's.

If the collector has little money to expend he will have to try to find the material himself by dint of haunting antique shops, junk shops, antiquarian booksellers, going to sales of the contents of houses; and above all, publishing his interest to all and sundry.

Correct identification of autographs is of primary importance and confusion is easy. For example, Sir Robert Peel and his son had similar handwriting and similar signatures. So, unless the letter was dated, which it might well not be as both men frequently omitted the date, there would be little, except perhaps the content and the addressee to indicate which was the writer. Fortunately, the writing paper of the 19th century was often watermarked with the date which could help a lot in a case like this. But the first step towards correct identification must normally lie in the signature and the writing itself. There have been a number of books of autograph facsimiles published over the last 150 years and these are invaluable to the collector. Though most are out of print they can still be found through secondhand or antiquarian booksellers and, on occasions, through autograph dealers.

Forgeries and facsimiles exist in plenty, especially the latter. Only experience and the use of a facsimile book will help to detect forgeries, though the more obvious ones may well be reproduced on the wrong kind of paper, or show watermarks which were not in use at the time the subject was living and/or fail to accord with the date of the letter. Facsimiles are a question of 'look' and these can be very deceiving. For instance, a modern xerox copy, if it is of a letter on pure white paper, can look extremely 'real' at first, or even second, glance. Some older facsimiles can be equally difficult to detect and the collector would be strongly advised to get a second opinion from an expert if he has any doubts. The use of autopen and secretarial signatures is referred to in the Preface.

Finally a short word about preservation. Never cut an autograph down. It will lessen its value and if a signature is cut off a letter it can destroy the value both of the signature and of the letter. Never stick autographs directly down into books or on to mounts. Keep them in loose-leafed transparent envelopes or between boards or in files but never glued, fastened or stapled into these.

I keep my own in envelopes transparent in front with plain white backing. These envelopes I hinge into large leather-covered volumes specially made with guards between the pages to avoid their fanning out and becoming misshapen when full. The autograph can be seen through the transparent front and removed easily for examination or should it be required to read any continuation pages.

Do not frame autographs under ordinary glass unless you keep them well away from light because glass can make them sweat and, of course, light which easily penetrates ordinary glass, will fade them. Do not attempt repairs yourself except very elementary ones and even then never use any form of sticky tape which will be likely to eat into the paper. It is best, in fact, to leave the item well alone unless it is so torn or creased that it becomes unreadable, under which circumstances a professional repairer should be employed.

Keep a record of your collection. An index is essential. And wherever you keep your autographs make sure that you indicate whose they are. *You* know who has written every item in your collection but those who follow you will not thank you if they cannot read an indecipherable autograph which you have failed to name.

Keep your autographs in some sort of regular order, by countries, by professions, by periods of history or in historical or alphabetical order. This may become difficult as your collection grows but some sort of sequence will make them easier to handle and of more interest to the observer. I am sure Henry VIII would like to have been close to Marilyn Monroe had they been contemporaries but their juxtaposition in any autograph collection would be, to say the least, inappropriate.

INDEX OF CROSS REFERENCES

ABDUL-HAMID II, 1842–1918. Last Sultan of Turkey. His long reign of misrule and withholding of reforms culminated in his being deposed by the Turkish Parliament and exiled in 1909.

ABDULLAH IBN HUSSEIN, 1882–1951. First King of Jordan 1946–51. With **T E Lawrence** and Faisal led the successful Arab revolt against the Turks in World War I. Emir of Transjordan 1921–46.

ABERDEEN, George Gordon, 4th Earl of 1784–1860. British statesman. Prime Minister 1852–5.
See also signature with British Prime Ministers page 69.

ADAMS, John 1735–1826. American statesman. Succeeded **Washington** as (2nd) President of the USA 1797–1801.
See also signature with US Presidents page 204.

ADAMS, John Quincy 1767–1848. Sixth President of the USA 1825–29. Son of President **John Adams**.
See also signature with US Presidents page 204.

ADDISON, Joseph 1672–1719. English essayist and poet.
Addison's signature can be found on certain official documents as he held several state appointments.

ADENAUER, Konrad 1876–1967. Chancellor of the German Federal Republic 1949–63. Played a major part in the rebuilding of his country after World War II.

ADLER, Alfred 1870–1937. Austrian psychiatrist. Developed 'Individual Psychology'. Celebrated for his theory of 'inferiority complex'.

AGASSIZ, (Jean) Louis (Rodolfe) 1807–73. Swiss-born American naturalist. Professor of Natural History at Harvard University. Variant signatures.

ALANBROOKE, Alan F Brooke, Viscount 1883–1963. British Field Marshal. As Chief of the Imperial General Staff he was **Churchill**'s senior strategic adviser in World War II.

ALBA (or **ALVA**), Ferdinand Alvarez de Toledo, Duke of 1508–82. Spanish soldier. Successful under **Charles V**, he later suppressed the Netherlands with great cruelty.

ALBERT, Prince 1819–61. The Prince Consort. Husband of Queen **Victoria**. Son of the Duke of Saxe-Coburg-Gotha. An active patron of the arts and sciences.

ALBERT I, 1875–1934. King of the Belgians 1909–34. In World War I he led his country's resistance to the Germans and earned worldwide admiration for his conduct during the occupation of Belgium.

ALBUQUERQUE, Affonso d' 1453–1515. Called 'The Great'. Founded the Portuguese Eastern empire (Goa, Ceylon, Malacca, etc.) and was Viceroy from 1506.

ALCOCK, Sir John W 1892–1919. British pioneer aviator. First to fly across the Atlantic, 14 June 1919 with **Sir Arthur Whitten Brown**.
The signatures of Alcock and Brown are shown together. That of Alcock is extremely rare as he was killed in an aeroplane accident only six months after his historic flight.

ALCOTT, Louisa May 1832–88. American author of children's classics, such as *Little Women*.

ALEKHIN(E), Alexander 1892–1946. Russian-born, French-naturalised world chess champion.

ALEXANDER I, 1777–1825. Tsar of Russia 1801–25. A principal opponent of **Napoleon**.
Signatures in both French and Russian styles.

ALEXANDER III, 1845–94. Tsar of Russia 1881–94. A reactionary ruler, he was both anti-liberal and anti-Jewish.

ALEXANDER VI, Rodrigo Borgia 1431–1503. Father of **Cesare** and **Lucrezia Borgia**. 215th Pope 1492–1503. Died after drinking from a cup intended for one of his own guests.

ALEXANDER OF TUNIS, Harold R L, 1st Earl 1891–1969. Supreme Allied Commander, Mediterranean Theatre, World World II. Governor-General of Canada 1946–52.

ALFIERI, Count Vittorio 1749–1803. One of Italy's greatest poet-dramatists. He lived for many years with the Countess of Albany, the estranged wife of **Charles Edward Stuart**, 'the Young Pretender'.

ALFONSO V, 1385–1458. King of Aragon, Sicily and Naples. Known as 'the Magnanimous'.
Rare signature as 'Rex Alfonsus' on a document permitting the practice of medicine and surgery by Maestro Angelo, Naples, 18 June 1456. (Author's Collection.)

ALFONSO XIII, 1886–1941. Last King of Spain. Born a king, the posthumous son of Alfonso XII, he was deposed in 1931. Variant signatures: private as 'Alfonso' and official as 'Yo El Rey' ('I the King').

ALI, Muhammed b. 1942. American boxer. Heavyweight champion of the world. Formerly known as Cassius Clay. Ali's signature varies considerably. This example is only comparatively typical.

ALLENBY, Edmund H H, Viscount 1861–1936. British Field-Marshal. Commanded in the successful campaign against the Turks in Palestine, World War I.

AMPÈRE, André Marie 1775–1836. French physicist, mathematician and electrical scientist. A pioneer of electrodynamics. The unit of electrical current intensity, the 'amp', is named after him.

AMUNDSEN, Roald E G 1872–1928. Norwegian polar explorer. First man to reach the South Pole, 14 December 1911.

ANDERSEN, Hans Christian 1805–75. Danish author. Famed for his *Fairy Tales*. Examples of his autograph in Danish and English, the latter written when visiting **Dickens** at Gad's Hill, in which he quotes a line from **Longfellow**. The connection between Andersen and Dickens adds to the autographic interest of this item. (Author's Collection.)

ANDERSON, Paul b. 1933. American weightlifter. Olympic heavyweight champion 1956. Lifted the greatest weight ever raised by a human being, 6270 lb (2844 kg) in 1957.

ANNE, 1665–1714. Queen of Great Britain and Ireland 1702–14.
See also signature with British Sovereigns page 25.

ANNE OF AUSTRIA, 1601–66. Queen Consort of **Louis XIII** of France and later Queen Regent for the infant **Louis XIV**.

ANNE BOLEYN, 1504–36. Queen and second wife of **Henry VIII**. Mother of **Elizabeth I**. Beheaded 1536.
See also under HENRY VIII.

ANNE OF CLEVES, 1515–57. Fourth wife of **Henry VIII** 1540. Marriage annulled after six months.
See also under HENRY VIII.

ANNIGONI, Pietro b. 1910. Italian painter distinguished for the Renaissance style of his portraits as in that of **Queen Elizabeth II** (1955).

ANOUILH, Jean b. 1910. Leading modern French dramatist. Works include *Antigone*, *Becket* and *L'Alouette*.

APOLLINAIRE, Guillaume (originally W Appollinaris de Kostrowitsky) 1880–1918. French poet and writer of Polish descent whose work is associated with cubism and exoticism. A much sought-after autograph.

ARCHER, Frederick James 1857–86. British champion jockey who won the Derby five times. His early suicide causes his autograph, shown here with his name device, an archer, to be scarce.

ARIOSTO, Ludovico 1474–1533. Italian Renaissance poet, dramatist and satirist. His masterpiece is the Roland epic poem *Orlando Furioso*.

A

ARKWRIGHT, Sir Richard 1732–92. English inventor of the spinning frame which revolutionised the cotton industry.

ARMSTRONG, Louis 1900–71. 'Satchmo'. American jazz trumpeter, singer and band leader.

ARMSTRONG, Neil A b. 1930. American astronaut. The first man to set foot on the Moon, 21 July 1969. Signature. Also a photograph of Aldrin on the Moon taken and signed by Armstrong; also signed by Col. E. E. ('Buzz') Aldrin and Lt. Col. Michael Collins, his fellow astronauts in the first lunar conquest. (NASA photo.) (Author's Collection.)

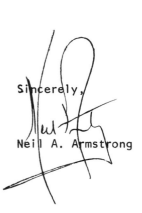

Sincerely,

Neil A. Armstrong

ARNOLD, Matthew 1822–88. Poet and critic. Son of **Thomas Arnold**. ALS expressing interesting views on Catholicism, 1888. (Author's Collection.) Arnold held an appointment as an Inspector of Schools for 35 years so that it is possible to find his autograph on certain government papers connected with education.

6

ARNOLD, Thomas 1795–1842. English educationalist, scholar and historian. As Headmaster of Rugby School, he re-organised the public school system. Immortalised by **Thomas Hughes** in *Tom Brown's Schooldays*.

ARTHUR, Chester Alan 1830–88. Twenty-first President of the USA.
See also signature with US Presidents page 205.

ASQUITH, Herbert Henry, Earl of Oxford and 1852–1928. British statesman.
See also with British Prime Ministers page 69.

ASTAIRE, Fred b. 1899. American dancer and film actor. His first partner was his sister Adele, later Lady Charles Cavendish. Subsequently, he starred in a series of immensely popular film 'musicals' partnered by Ginger Rogers.

ATATÜRK, Mustafa Kemal 1881–1938. Turkish soldier, statesman and President. Scarce signature before adding his self-chosen surname 'Atatürk' and incorporating his popular title of 'Gazi' ('Leader').

ATTLEE, Clement, 1st Earl 1883–1967. British Socialist statesman. Prime Minister 1945–51.
See also signature with British Prime Ministers page 69.

AUBER, Daniel (François-Esprit) 1782–1871. French operatic composer of *Fra Diavolo*, etc. Auber was a pupil of **Cherubini**.
ALS concerning tickets for a performance. (Author's Collection.)

AUDEN, W(ystan) H(ugh) 1907 73. British-born, American-naturalised poet. Auden's autograph is in demand and is fairly scarce.

AUDUBON, John James 1785–1851. American ornithologist. Produced classic books on birds.
Autographically, particularly in the USA, highly desirable.

AUGEREAU, Pierre F C, Duke of Castiglione 1757–1816. French Marshal. A renowned swordsman.
See also Napoleonic Marshals page 178.

AURIOL, Vincent 1884–1966. French Socialist statesman. President of France 1947–53.

AUSTEN, Jane 1775–1817. English novelist. Famed for *Pride and Prejudice*, *Northanger Abbey*, etc. Her holograph Will dated 27 April 1817. (Public Record Office, London.)

AUSTIN, Herbert, Lord 1866–1941. English motor-car manufacturer. Produced his first car in 1895.
See pig drawn blindfold page 147.

AYUB KHAN, Mohammed 1907–74. Pakistani statesman and Field Marshal. First C-in-C, Pakistan Army 1951. President 1958–69.

BACH, Johann Sebastian 1685–1750. German composer. One of the greatest names in music.

Variant autographs. Also holograph music.

BACKHAUS, Wilhelm 1884–1969. German pianist. Winner of the Rubinstein prize.

BACON, Sir Francis, Baron Verulam and Viscount St Albans 1561–1626. English statesman, philosopher and author. A considerable school of thought believes him to be the author of the plays attributed to **Shakespeare**.

Variant autographs including one as 'Fr(anciscus) Verulam Canc(ellarius)' = 'Francis Verulam Chancellor' signed when Lord Chancellor.

BADEN-POWELL, Robert, Lord 1857–1941. British soldier. Founder of the Boy Scouts and Girl Guides.

Also see pig drawn blindfold page 147.

BAFFIN, William 1584–1622. English navigator. His voyage as far as latitude 77°45′ created a record not eclipsed for 236 years. Baffin Bay and Baffin Island are named after him.

BAILEY, Sir Abe 1864–1940. South African financier and mining millionaire.

BAIRD, John Logie 1888–1946. Scottish television inventor. Gave the first demonstration of a televised image, 1926. An uncommon autograph.

BAKER, Sir Samuel White 1821–93. British explorer and soldier. Explored the Nile and discovered Lake Albert (Nyanza).
Extract from an ALS with a humorous forthright comment on a military appointment.

BAKUNIN, Michael 1814–76. Russian anarchist and writer of aristocratic descent. Opposed **Karl Marx** and was expelled from the First Communist International.

BALBOA, Vasco Nuñez de 1475–1517. Spanish navigator and discoverer of the Pacific Ocean in 1513.

BALDWIN, Stanley, Earl 1867–1947. British statesman. Thrice Prime Minister. PS. (Author's Collection.)
See also with British Prime Ministers page 69.

BALFOUR, Arthur James, Earl 1848–1930. British statesman and philosopher. Premier 1902–5.
See also with British Prime Ministers page 69.

BALZAC, Honoré de 1799–1850. One of France's greatest novelists. Two examples of his sought-after autograph, one showing the shortened signature he frequently used.

BANDA, H Kamuzu b. 1905. First Prime Minister, 1963 and first President, 1966 of Malawi (formerly Nyasaland).

BANDARANAIKE, Sirimavu b. 1916. Widow of the assassinated Prime Minister of Ceylon (now Sri Lanka). She was herself Premier 1960–5 and again 1970–7. PS. (Author's Collection.)

BANKS, Sir Joseph 1743–1820. English naturalist and botanist. Accompanied **Cook** on his round-the-world voyage. A founder of the Australian state of New South Wales.

BANNISTER, Sir Roger (Gilbert) b. 1929. British athlete. The first man to run the mile in under four minutes (Oxford, 6 May 1954).
A notification of selection to represent Oxford University Centipede Athletic Club, signed as the Club's Hon. Secretary. (Author's Collection.)

OXFORD UNIVERSITY CENTIPEDE ATHLETIC CLUB

You have been selected to represent the Club .... against .... Sandhurst .... at ...... Cowley .... on .... 31st May .... in the following event(s) .... 220yds ....

TRAVELLING.
Coach leaves B.N... 12·15

If you are unable to accept this invitation will you please notify me at once at .... Exeter .... College.

R.G. Bannister
Hon. Sec. O.U.C.A.C.

B

BANTING, Sir Frederick Grant 1891–1941. Canadian doctor. In 1923 won the Nobel Prize for his discovery (with **Charles H Best**) of insulin, used in the treatment of diabetes.

BARNA, G Viktor 1912–72. Hungarian table tennis player. Won fifteen world championship titles.

BARNARD, Christiaan Neethling b. 1922. South African surgeon. Performed the first human heart transplant operation, December 1967.

BARNUM, Phineas Taylor 1810–91. American showman. Proprietor of 'The Greatest Show on Earth'.

BARRAS, Paul Jean F N, Comte de 1755–1829. French Revolutionary and at one time virtual dictator of France. He 'sponsored' **Napoleon Bonaparte**.

BARRIE, Sir James M 1860–1937. Scottish novelist and dramatist. Remembered as the creator of *Peter Pan*. Often used an amanuensis whose writing was rather similar to his own.

BARRYMORE, Ethel 1879–1959. American actress. Sister of the actor brothers John and Lionel Barrymore.

BART, Jean 1651–1702. French sailor and soldier of fortune. The daring exploits of this one-time privateer made him a national hero.

BARTH, Karl 1886–1968. Swiss Protestant theologian. A philosopher himself, he expressed an anti-philosophical theology.

BARTÓK, Béla 1881–1945. Hungarian composer.
Bartók's autograph, as with many composers, is sought after.

BATH, William Pulteney, Earl of 1684–1764. British statesman. Held office as Prime Minister for three days, 10–12 February 1746.
See also signature with British Prime Ministers page 68.

BAUDELAIRE, Charles Pierre 1821–67. French poet. Translated the poems of **Edgar Allan Poe**.
Baudelaire's autograph is much sought after.

BAYARD, Pierre du Terrail, Chevalier de 1476–1524. French military hero. The almost legendary 'knight without fear and without reproach'.

BAYLE, Pierre 1647–1706. French philosopher. An exponent of religious tolerance. Author of the celebrated *Dictionnaire historique et critique*. Note. His signature is much larger than the rest of his writing.

BEAMON, Robert b. 1946. American athlete. Set a world record of 8·90 m (29 ft 2½ in.) in the Long Jump at Mexico City Olympics, 1968.

BEARDSLEY, Aubrey 1872–98. English illustrator and poster artist.
Beardsley's autograph is rare because of his very early death.
ALS re an entry in *Who's Who*. (Richmond Borough Council Library.)

BEATLES, The. The fabulously successful 'Pop' group of the sixties – 'Ringo STARR' (real name Richard STARKEY) b. 1940, (James) Paul McCARTNEY b. 1942, John (Winston) LENNON b. 1940 and George HARRISON b. 1943. Lennon and McCartney were responsible as a team for more than 150 songs recorded by the Beatles. The most successful of these was 'Yesterday'. Other outstanding Beatle numbers include 'Can't Buy Me Love' and 'I Want to Hold Your Hand'.

PS by all (from *Name Dropper* by Peter Hildreth – McWhirter, 1970).

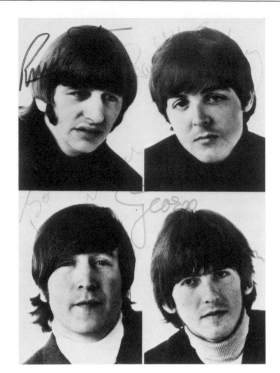

BEATTY, David, Earl 1871–1936. British Admiral of the Fleet. Commanded the Grand Fleet in World War I.

BEAVERBROOK, William Maxwell Aitken, 1st Lord 1879–1964. Canadian-born British newspaper proprietor and statesman.

BECKETT, Samuel b. 1906. Irish author and playwright (*Waiting for Godot*, etc.). Nobel Prize for literature 1969.

BEECHAM, Sir Thomas 1879–1961. British orchestral conductor and impresario. He was the son of Sir Joseph Beecham, the pill millionaire.

BEERBOHM, Sir H Max(imilian) 1872–1956. 'The Incomparable Max'. British humorist and caricaturist.

BEETHOVEN, Ludwig van 1770–1827. The great German composer.

Beethoven's signature varied considerably throughout his life. Examples in both Germanic and Italic script are shown together with part of the holograph score of his soprano solo cantata *Adelaide*. (The British Library.)

BELL, Alexander Graham 1847–1922. Scottish-born American inventor of the telephone. A tireless worker for the education of the deaf.

BELLINI, Giovanni *c.* 1430–1516. Italian painter. A great master of the Venetian school.

An example of his style in signing his paintings.

BELLINI, Vincenzo 1801–35. Italian composer. Operas include *Norma* and *La Sonnambula*.

Bellini's autograph is becoming scarce.

BELLOC, (J) Hilaire (P) 1870–1953. Anglo-French man of letters. Wrote books for children and on travel, history and religion.

BELOUSOVA, Ludmilla. Russian world ice-skating champion. Partnered by **Oleg Protopopov**.
See also under PROTOPOPOV.

BENEŠ, Eduard 1884–1948. Czechoslovak patriot and statesman. As a disciple of **Masaryk**, helped to found the state of Czechoslovakia after World War I and was twice its President.

BEN-GURION, David 1886–1973. Israeli statesman and patriot. First Prime Minister of Israel.

BENNETT, (E) Arnold 1867–1931. English novelist. Known in particular for his *Clayhanger* series of novels.

BENTHAM, Jeremy 1748–1832. English philosopher, jurist and writer on Utilitarian ethics. His skeleton, dressed in his own clothes is preserved in University College, London, which he founded.
Autograph verse written in the *album amicorum* of Sir John Bowring, the administrator, linguist and staunch Benthamite.
(Author's Collection.)

BENZ, Karl F 1844–1929. German pioneer of the petrol-driven vehicle, the motor car. Constructed a two-stroke model in 1879.
PS. (Daimler-Benz Museum.) Having started a factory for its manufacture and development he joined with the **Daimler** firm in 1926.

BÉRANGER, Pierre Jean de 1780–1857. French lyric poet famed for his *chansons*.

BERGMAN, Ingrid b. 1917. Swedish film actress. She has also taken part in stage plays in London, Paris and New York.

BERGSON, Henri 1859–1941. French philosopher. Won Nobel Prize for literature 1927. Works include *Matter and Memory* and *Time and Free Will*.

BERING, Vitus 1681–1741. Danish navigator. Bering Sea, Strait and Island (where he died after being shipwrecked) are all named after him.

BERKELEY, George 1685–1753. Irish philosopher. His philosophy influenced **Kant**.
An Anglican cleric, he signs here as Bishop of Cloyne.

BERLIN, Irving (formerly I BALINE) b. 1888. American composer of popular songs and musicals. Works include 'I'm Dreaming of a White Christmas' and *Annie Get Your Gun*.

BERLIOZ, Hector 1803–69. French composer. 'The greatest musical figure in the French romantic movement.' (*Concise Oxford Dictionary of Music*.)
See also (with **Chopin**) at page 46.

BERNADETTE, Saint 1844–79. Bernadette Soubirous who as a child claimed to have had visions of the Virgin Mary at Lourdes, now a shrine of pilgrimage. Became a nun and was canonised in 1933.

BERNHARDT, Sarah (Henriette R Bernard) 1844–1923. 'The Divine Sarah'. France's most famous actress. The greatest tragedienne of her time.

BERNINI, Giovanni Lorenzo 1598–1680. Italian baroque sculptor, architect and painter. His greatest works include the Borghese sculptures *The Rape of Proserpina*, *David* and *Apollo and Daphne*.

BERTHIER, (Louis) Alexandre. Prince de Neuchâtel and of Wagram 1753–1815. Napoleon's Chief-of-Staff.
See also Napoleonic Marshals page 178.

BESSIÈRES, Jean Baptiste, Duke of Istria 1766–1813. Marshal of the French Empire to which rank he rose from that of a private.
See also Napoleonic Marshals page 178.

BEST, Charles Herbert b. 1899. Canadian physiologist. Co-discoverer of insulin with Sir F Banting.

BETJEMAN, Sir John b. 1906. British poet and writer. Poet Laureate 1972. An example of his usual signature and an exuberant one on a letter to a friend.

BEVIN, Ernest 1881–1951. British Labour statesman. 'The dockers' K.C.'
See also signature with **Stalin**.

BHUTTO, Zulfikar Ali b. 1928. President of Pakistan 1971. Later Prime Minister. Removed from office by a military *coup*, July 1977.

BISMARCK, Otto E L, Prince von 1815–98. 'The Iron Chancellor'. The leading Prussian statesman, he was the architect of the unification of the German states under the Prussian King, **Wilhelm I**.

BIZET, 'Georges' (correctly Alexandre C L) 1838–75. French composer. Famed for his opera *Carmen*.
Bizet's autograph, due in part to his short life, is scarce.

BJÖRNSON, Björnstjerne 1832–1910. Norwegian Nobel Prizewinning poet, novelist and dramatist. He was also a theatre manager, newspaper editor and the writer of Norway's national anthem.

BLACKMORE, R(ichard) D(oddridge) 1825–1900. English novelist. Remembered for his masterpiece, the West Country classic, *Lorna Doone*.
Part of a long ALS discussing his work and referring to *Lorna Doone* 1875.
(Author's Collection.)

BLACKSTONE, Sir William 1723–80. English jurist. Famed for his great work *Commentaries on the Laws of England*.

BLAKE, Robert 1599–1657. Recognised as, after **Nelson**, the greatest naval commander in British history. His principal opponents were the Dutch admirals **Tromp** and **De Ruyter**.

BLAKE, William 1757–1827. English poet, painter and mystic.
An important and rare literary autograph.
(The British Library.)

BLAMEY, Sir Thomas 1884–1951. Australian soldier. The first to become a British Field Marshal. As C-in-C Allied Land Forces in Asia, received the Japanese surrender in 1945.

BLANCHARD, (Jean Pierre) François 1753–1809. French balloonist and inventor of the parachute. First (with John Jeffries) to cross the English Channel by balloon, 1785.

BLANKERS-KOEN, Francina ('Fanny') b. 1918. Dutch athlete. Winner of four Olympic titles, 1948.

B

BLASCO IBÁÑEZ, Vicente 1867–1928. Spanish novelist. Author of the classic novel of World War I, *The Four Horsemen of the Apocalypse*.

BLÉRIOT, Louis 1872–1936. French pioneer airman. Made the first aeroplane crossing of the English Channel, 1909, a feat which he performed in a monoplane of his own design.

BLIGH, William 1754–1817. English admiral. His harsh treatment of his crew led to the mutiny in his ship *The Bounty*, 1789. Later as Governor of New South Wales, Australia, he again had to face mutiny. Part of his holograph report of the *Bounty* mutiny.(Public Record Office, London.)

BLOK, Aleksandr Alexandrovich 1880–1921. Russian poet and dramatist. One of his major works was *The Twelve* which welcomed the Russian Revolution of 1917.

BLONDIN, Charles (real name J F Gravelet) 1824–97. French tightrope walker. Crossed Niagara Falls several times on a tightrope (blindfold with a wheelbarrow, with a man on his back, etc.).

BLÜCHER, Gebhard Leberecht von, Prince of Wahlstadt 1742–1819. Prussian soldier. Came to the assistance of **Wellington** at Waterloo 1815. Variant signatures.

BLUNDEN, Edmund (Charles) 1896–1974. English poet and critic. He also wrote books on other poets, notably **Lamb**, **Keats** and **Leigh Hunt**.

BOCCACCIO, Giovanni 1313–75. Italian Renaissance writer. Popularly remembered for his bawdy collection of tales, the *Decameron*.
Portion of an autograph MSS in the Biblioteca Laurentina, Florence (Zibaldone Laurenziano Plut. 29.8).

BÖHME (or BOEHME), Jakob 1575–1624. German mystic and theosophist. Particularly known for his great philosophical work *Aurora*.

BOHR, Niels H D 1885–1962. Danish physicist. Researched into atomic structure. Won Nobel Prize 1922.

BOITO, Arrigo 1842–1918. Italian composer, poet and librettist. Wrote the libretti for **Verdi**'s operas *Falstaff* and *Otello*. Shown here autograph music signed from Act II of his most famous opera *Mefistofele*. (Author's Collection.)

BOLÍVAR, Simon 1783–1830. 'The Liberator'. South American soldier, statesman and patriot. Responsible for the liberation of South America from Spanish rule. Bolivia named after him. Bolivar's autograph is scarce and greatly sought after. This signed example reads: 'A lovely lady has asked for (a lock of) my hair. I have given this to her.' (Author's Collection.)

BONHEUR, Rosa 1822–99. French painter, particularly of animals.

BONNARD, Pierre 1867–1947. French modernist painter. Examples (i) of his usual signature and (ii) that which he used on his paintings.

(i) (ii)

BOONE, Daniel 1734–1820. American pioneer frontiersman and folklore hero. The leading Indian fighter he was twice captured by them.

BOOTH, William 1829–1912. British founder and first 'General' of the Salvation Army, 1865.

BORGIA, Cesare 1476–1507. Italian soldier, statesman, cardinal and patron of art. Natural son of Pope **Alexander VI**.
His signature as Cardinal Archbishop of Valencia and as 'Cesar'.

BORGIA, Lucrezia 1480–1519. Sister of **Cesare Borgia**; daughter of Pope **Alexander VI**. Though her reputation is one of cruelty, vice and wantonness, this rests largely on her being a member of the notorious Borgia family. She was a patroness of art and learning. Her full signature (top) as acquiescing to the request of one of her 'servants' to be allowed to change his house, dated 16 March 1495 when she was only fifteen years old. The signature reads 'Lucrezia Sforza (her first married name) Borgia manu p(er) p(ropio) f(ecit)'. An extremely rare autograph. (Author's Collection.)

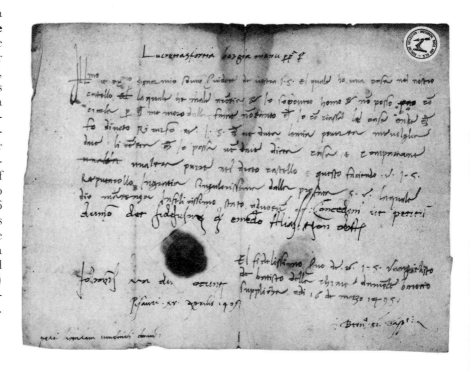

BORIS III, 1894–1943. King of Bulgaria 1918–43. Brought his country into World War II on the side of Germany.

BORN, Max 1882– 1970. German physicist. Won Nobel Prize for work on quantum physics, 1954.
The 'N.L.' after his signature stands for 'Nobel Laureate'.

BORODIN, Alexandr Porfirevich 1833–87. Russian composer. **Rimsky-Korsakov** completed his unfinished opera *Prince Igor*. Also a physician and chemist.
Variant signature examples.

BOROTRA, Jean b. 1898. French tennis player, particularly successful in the Davis Cup matches 1925–32.
Autograph on his visiting card.

BORUWLASKI, Josef, 'Count' 1739–1837. Celebrated Polish midget. His height altered from 35 in (89 cm) at 25 years to 39 in (99 cm) at 30. Also remarkable for his long life, exceptional for a dwarf, of almost 98 years.

BOSCH, Hieronymus (Also Jerom Bos or van Aken) 1460–1516. Dutch painter known for his fantastic and macabre paintings of devils, monsters, etc. Examples of the way in which he signed his work.

BOSWELL, James 1740–95. Scottish writer and lawyer. Friend and disciple of Dr **Samuel Johnson**, his fame lies in his *Life* of that great man.

BOTHA, Louis 1862–1919. South African soldier and statesman. Commander of the Boer Forces in the South African War, he became the first Prime Minister of the Union of South Africa, 1910.

BOTTICELLI, Sandro 1444–1510. Florentine painter. Botticelli's usual autograph is almost unknown. An example of his method of signing paintings, the initials 'S.B.', together with a full signature which is probably not his but that of the 16th-century artist Pierre François Botticelli.

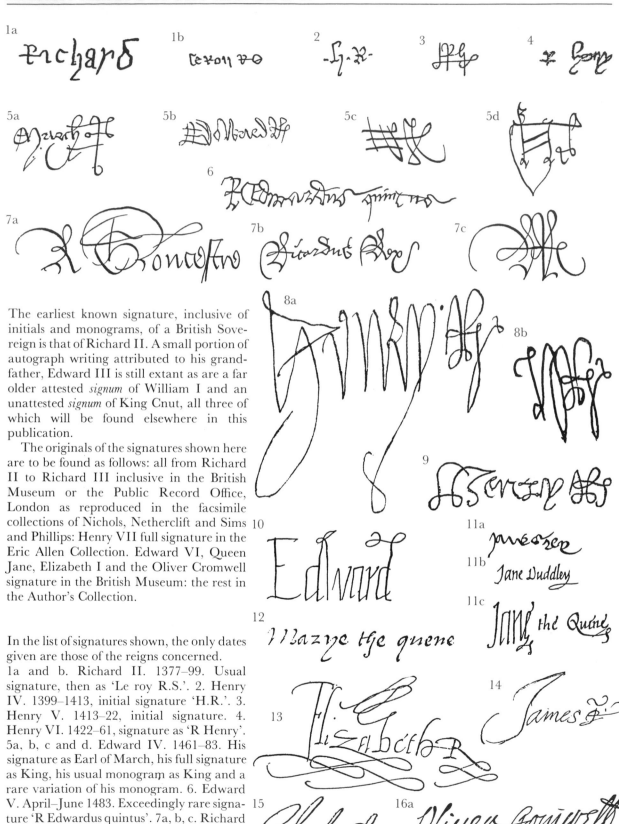

The earliest known signature, inclusive of initials and monograms, of a British Sovereign is that of Richard II. A small portion of autograph writing attributed to his grandfather, Edward III is still extant as are a far older attested *signum* of William I and an unattested *signum* of King Cnut, all three of which will be found elsewhere in this publication.

The originals of the signatures shown here are to be found as follows: all from Richard II to Richard III inclusive in the British Museum or the Public Record Office, London as reproduced in the facsimile collections of Nichols, Netherclift and Sims and Phillips: Henry VII full signature in the Eric Allen Collection. Edward VI, Queen Jane, Elizabeth I and the Oliver Cromwell signature in the British Museum: the rest in the Author's Collection.

In the list of signatures shown, the only dates given are those of the reigns concerned.
1a and b. Richard II. 1377–99. Usual signature, then as 'Le roy R.S.'. 2. Henry IV. 1399–1413, initial signature 'H.R.'. 3. Henry V. 1413–22, initial signature. 4. Henry VI. 1422–61, signature as 'R Henry'. 5a, b, c and d. Edward IV. 1461–83. His signature as Earl of March, his full signature as King, his usual monogram as King and a rare variation of his monogram. 6. Edward V. April–June 1483. Exceedingly rare signature 'R Edwardus quintus'. 7a, b, c. Richard III. 1483–5. Signatures as Duke of Gloucester and as King and monogram as King. 8a

16b 17 18

19 20 21 22

23 24 25a 26

25b 27 28 29 30 31a 32 31b 33

and b. Henry VII. 1485–1509. Full signature and his more commonly used monogram. 9. Henry VIII. 1509–47. 10. Edward VI. 1547–53. His signature is very rare. 11a, b and c. Jane, known as Lady Jane Grey. 9–19 July 1553. Signatures as 'Jane Grey' (using old secretary hand), 'Jane Dudley' and as Queen. 12. Mary I. 1553–8. 13. Elizabeth I. 1558–1603. 14. James I (James VI of Scotland). 1603–25. 15. Charles I. 1625–49. 16a and b. Oliver Cromwell. 1653–8. Signatures before and during his protectorate. 17. Richard Cromwell. 1658–9. Scarce signature as Protector. 18. Charles II. 1660 (restored)–85. 19. James II. 1685–8. 20 and 21. William III, 1689–1702, and Mary II. 1689–94. 22. Anne. 1702–14. 23. George I. 1714–27. 24. George II. 1727–60. 25a and b. George III. 1760–1820. The signature he used in the first few years of his reign and his usual signature thereafter. When he became blind and at times insane, George III's signature varied considerably, becoming ill-formed and even illegible. 26. George IV. 1820–30. 27. William IV. 1830–7. Before his accession he signed as 'Clarence', his ducal title. 28. Queen Victoria. 1837–1901. 29. Edward VII. 1901–10. 30. George V. 1910–36. 31a and b. Edward VIII. 20 January–11 December 1936. His signature as Prince of Wales and as King. The latter, owing to his very short reign, is becoming scarce. After his abdication he signed 'Edward, Duke of Windsor'. 32. George VI. 1936–52. Before coming to the throne, he signed 'Albert' as Duke of York. 33. Elizabeth II. 1952–.

BOUGAINVILLE, Louis Antoine de 1729–1811. French mariner. Commanded the first French circumnavigation of the world.
An example of his scarce holograph.

BRADLEY, Omar Nelson b. 1893. American General. Led the US Army in the invasion of France 1944. Chairman of the Joint Chiefs of Staff 1949.

BRADMAN, Sir Donald G b. 1908. Australian cricketer who set many batting records, including the greatest number of centuries scored in Test matches, 29 between 1928 and 1948.

BRAGG, Sir William H 1862–1942. British Nobel Prizewinning physicist. Worked on the study of radioactivity, X-rays and crystals.

BRAGG, Sir W Lawrence 1890–1971. British physicist. Son of **Sir William H Bragg** with whom he won the Nobel Prize in 1915 for work on the theory of X-ray diffraction.

BRAHE, Tycho 1546–1601. Danish astronomer. Established his Observatory on Hven Island, 1576, where he worked for twenty years. Later, he worked in Bohemia. **Kepler** was one of his assistants.

BRAHMS, Johannes 1833–97. Famed German composer and pianist. Examples of his full and initial signatures (he frequently employed the latter) and of his holograph music.

BRANDT, Willy b. 1913. German Social Democratic statesman. Chancellor of (West) Germany 1969. Formerly Mayor of West Berlin.

BRAQUE, Georges 1882–1963. French painter. One of the founders of cubism. An example of his signature on his paintings.

BRECHT, (Eugen) Bertholt 1898–1956. German dramatist and poet.
Variant signatures (i) 1919 (ii) 1932.

BREZHNEV, Leonid Ilych b. 1906. Soviet statesman. President of the Praesidium 1960–64. First Secretary of the Communist Central Committee in succession to **Khrushchev** 1964. President 1977.

BRIAND, Aristide 1862–1932. French Socialist statesman. Eleven times Prime Minister. Winner of the 1926 Nobel Peace Prize.
Holograph writing on his visiting card.

BRIDGES, Robert (S) 1844–1930. British Poet Laureate (1913). He was a qualified physician and also a dramatist, critic and advocate of spelling reform.

BRITTEN, (Edward) Benjamin, Lord 1913–76. Major British composer. Operas include *Billy Budd* and *Peter Grimes*.

BRONTË, Anne 1820–49. Pseudonym 'Acton Bell'. Poet and novelist. The youngest of the three literary Brontë sisters.
Her dated initials and part of the holograph MS of a poem commencing: 'Believe not those who say the upward path is smooth'. (The British Library.)

BRONTË, Charlotte 1816–55. Pseudonym 'Currer Bell'. Novelist and poet. The eldest of the three Brontë sisters. Famed for her novel *Jane Eyre*.
Portion of an ALS. (Author's Collection.) Also part of the holograph of *Jane Eyre*. (The British Library.) Charlotte Brontë's autograph is scarce and highly sought after. Autographs of her two sisters are very rare.

BRONTË, Emily (Jane) 1818–48. Pseudonym 'Ellis Bell'. The second of the three literary sisters. The author of *Wuthering Heights*.
Part of the original MS of her poem *Remembrance*. (The British Library.)

BROOKE, Rupert (Chawner) 1887–1915. English poet.
Owing to his early death whilst on active service, Brooke's autograph is scarce.

BROWN, Sir Arthur Whitten 1886–1948. Flew with **Alcock** on the first trans-Atlantic flight, 1919.
See also under ALCOCK.

BROWN, John 1800–1859. American abolitionist. Hanged for treason but held by many to be a martyr: hence the song 'John Brown's body lies a-mouldering in the grave'.

BROWNING, Elizabeth Barrett 1806–61. English poet. Wife of **Robert Browning**. Elizabeth Browning's autograph is much more scarce than that of her husband.

BROWNING, Robert 1812–89. English poet who married Elizabeth Barrett. Usual signature and part of an ALS bearing a hurried and more unusual example. (Author's Collection.)

BRUCE, Sir David 1855–1931. Australian-born British bacteriologist who discovered the cause of sleeping sickness, the tsetse fly.

BRUCE, Stanley Melbourne, Viscount 1883–1967. Australian statesman. Prime Minister 1923–9.

BRUCH, Max 1838–1920. German composer. Also distinguished as a conductor.

BRUEGEL (BREUGEL, BREUGHEL or BRUEGHEL), Pieter, the Elder, 1520–69. Flemish genre painter mostly of lively peasant scenes.
Variant signatures from his paintings.

BRUEGEL (BREUGEL, BREUGHEL or BRUEGHEL), Pieter, the Younger 1564–1637. Flemish painter. Known as 'Hell Bruegel' for his paintings of devils, hell, hags and scenes of pain and grief. Variant signatures.

BRUMMELL, George Bryan 1778–1840. 'Beau Brummell'. The famous 'Dandy'. Leader of English fashion during the Regency.
An ALS to his tailor. (Author's Collection.)

BRUNE, Guillaume M A 1763–1815. French Marshal of the Empire.
See also Napoleonic Marshals page 178.

BRUNEL, Isambard Kingdom 1806–59. English engineer. Son of **Sir Marc I Brunel**. Built the Clifton Suspension Bridge and the first steamship to cross the Atlantic, the *Great Western*; also the *Great Eastern*, then the largest steamship ever constructed.
Part of an ALS concerning his work force. Brunel's writing is almost unreadable.

BRUNEL, Sir Marc Isambard 1769–1849. French-born English engineer. Father of the foregoing. Built the Thames Tunnel, etc. In complete contrast to that of his son (above) M. I. Brunel's writing is most readable.

BUBER, Martin 1878–1965. Austrian Jewish theologian and philosopher. A religious existentialist, he was influenced by the works of **Kierkegaard**.

BUCHANAN, James 1791–1868. Fifteenth President of the USA.
See also with Presidents of the USA page 204.

BUCHINGER, Mathew 1674–? German artist and calligrapher without hands, feet or thighs. So remarkable is his work that some of it is preserved in the famous Harleian Collection at the British Museum.
An example of his calligraphy. (Author's Collection.)

BUCK, Pearl S 1892–1973. American novelist. Wrote *The Good Earth*, etc. Nobel Literature Prize 1938.

BUCKINGHAM, George Villiers, First Duke of 1592–1628. English statesman. Favourite of **James I**.
Usual signature and as 'Steenie' (nickname).

BUFFON, Georges L L Comte de 1707–88. French naturalist. Director of the Jardin du Roi, 1739, he was the chief compiler of the 44-volume *Histoire Naturelle*.
A sought-after French scientific autograph.

BÜLOW, Baron Hans G von 1830–94. German pianist, conductor and composer. He married **Liszt**'s daughter Cosima who deserted him for **Wagner**.

BUNSEN, Robert Wilhelm 1811–99. German chemist and physicist. Invented the 'Bunsen burner'. A discoverer of spectrum analysis and of the elements rubidium and caesium.

BUNYAN, John 1628–88. English preacher and writer. Author of *Pilgrim's Progress*. A very rare autograph.

BURGHLEY, William Cecil, Lord 1520–98. The outstanding British statesman of the Tudor Age. Chief Secretary of State and for 40 years leading counsellor of **Elizabeth I**.

BURGOYNE, John 1722–92. Soldier and dramatist. Otherwise a successful military commander, forced to surrender at Saratoga during the American War of Independence. Wrote the comedy *The Heiress*.

BURKE, Edmund 1729–97. Probably the most distinguished British statesman never to have held a senior Government appointment. Also a philosopher and powerful orator.

BURNS, Robert 1759–96. The Scottish poet.
Signed portion of a holograph poem. Burns' autograph, not strictly rare, is very much in demand.

BURNSIDE, Ambrose Everett 1824–81. American soldier after whom side-whiskers were named 'burnsides', now 'sideburns'. See also Dictionary names page 110.

BURR, Aaron 1756–1836. Controversial American statesman. Vice-President of the USA 1801–5. At one time he sought to create a new Republic in the South-west for which he was tried but acquitted.

BURROUGHS, Edgar Rice 1875–1950. American novelist. The creator of *Tarzan (of the Apes)*.

BURTON, Sir Richard (Francis) 1829–90. English explorer and Orientalist. Joint discoverer of Lake Tanganyika. Translated the *Arabian Nights*.
ANS. (Author's Collection.)

BUSTAMANTE, Sir (William) Alexander 1884–1977. First Prime Minister, 1962–7 of the independent state of Jamaica.

BUTE, John Stuart, 3rd Earl of 1713–92. British statesman and Premier.
See also signature with British Prime Ministers page 68.

BUTLER, Samuel 1835–1902. English man of letters. His masterpiece is the satirical *Erewhon*, 1872.
See also under BYRON.

BYRD, Richard Evelyn 1888–1957. American Polar explorer and Admiral. The first man to fly over the North Pole, 1926, he also flew over the South Pole, 1929 and led five Antarctic expeditions.

BYRON, George Gordon, 6th Lord. English poet 1788–1824.
Variant signatures. Also the cover of a letter bearing his franking signature addressed to the philosopher-divine Samuel Butler (1774–1839). On the flap of the cover is a holograph initialled note by the writer **Samuel Butler**, the grandson of the addressee. (Author's Collection.)

CABOT, Sebastian *c.* 1474–1557. Venetian navigator, explorer and cartographer. Served **Ferdinand V** of Spain, the Emperor **Charles V** and **Henry VIII** of England. Explored the La Plata and made a map of the world. Part of a letter to Juan de Samano. (Harisse).

CALDERÓN DE LA BARCA, Pedro 1600–81. One of Spain's greatest dramatists, described by Schlegel as 'the fourth of a mighty quarternion, with Homer, Dante and Shakespeare'.

CALLAGHAN, (Leonard) James b. 1912. British Labour statesman. Served as Chancellor of the Exchequer, Home Secretary and Foreign Secretary before becoming Prime Minister, 1976. See also with British Prime Ministers page 69.

CALLAS, Maria M b. 1923. American operatic soprano of Greek parentage.

CALVIN, John 1509–64. French theologian and religious reformer. Established a theocratic government in Geneva.
Autograph with variant signatures.

CAMPBELL, Sir Malcolm 1885–1949. British racing motorist. Established world land and water speed records.

CAMPBELL, (Ignatius) Roy (D) 1901–57. South African poet. Works include *The Flaming Terrapin* and his autobiography *Light on a Dark Horse*. Seen here with three other South African authors. Left to right: Laurens **van der Post**, Alan **Paton**, Roy Campbell, Uys **Krige**. A rare photograph of what is probably the only occasion of their having all been together, signed by all four. Photo *Natal Mercury*. (Author's Collection.)

CAMPBELL, Thomas 1777–1844. Scots poet. Also a prominent journalist, his poems include 'Ye Mariners of England'.

CAMPBELL-BANNERMAN, Sir Henry 1836–1908. British statesman. See also with British Prime Ministers page 69.

CANALETTO, Antonio Canale, called 1697–1768. Venetian painter.
Care must be taken not to confuse his signature with that of his nephew Bernard Bellotto also called Canaletto.

Signatures of both artists.

CANNING, George 1770–1827. English statesman.
See also with British Prime Ministers page 68.

CANO, Juan Sebastian del (also Elcano) *c.* 1476–1526. Spanish sailor. The first circumnavigator (1522). Sailed with **Magellan** and took over command on his death.

CANOVA, Antonio 1757–1822. Venetian sculptor. Founder of the modern classic school of Italian sculpture.

C

CARDIGAN, James T Brudenell, 7th Earl of 1797–1868. English soldier who led the charge of the Light Brigade at Balaklava. See also with Dictionary names page 110.

CARDUCCI, Giosuè 1835–1907. Italian poet. Winner of the Nobel Literature Prize 1906. Widely differing signatures, (i) from Geigy's Album (ii) from an ALS 1902 (Saggiori Catalogue).

CARLOS I, King 1863–1908. Last King of Portugal. Assassinated.
Also see pig drawn blindfold at page 147.

CARLOS III, King 1716–88. King of Spain 1759–88.
Signature as 'Yo el Rey' – 'I the King'.

CARLYLE, Thomas 1795–1881. Scottish historian and man of letters.
An amusing example of an invitation acceptance. ALS referring to the 'poisonous weather' and to his having 'the palsiest set of nerves in the world'. (Author's Collection.)

CARMAN, William Bliss 1861–1929. Canadian poet and essayist. Wrote nature verse such as *Low Tide on Grand Pré*.

CARNEGIE, Andrew 1835–1918. Scottish-born industrialist and philanthropist in USA. Endowed the Carnegie Institutes and Libraries throughout the world.

CARNERA, Primo 1906–67. 'The Ambling Alp'. Italian heavyweight champion boxer. The heaviest and tallest boxer ever to hold a world title. He also had the biggest chest, the longest reach and the largest fists.

CARNOT, Lazarre N M 1753–1823. French Revolutionary statesman and general. 'The Organiser (or Architect) of Victory'.

CARROLL, Lewis, pseudonym of Charles Lutgwidge Dodgson 1832–98. English author and mathematician. Famed for his children's classics *Alice in Wonderland* and *Alice Through the Looking Glass.*

Examples of both forms of his signature. Also part of the first MS of *Alice in Wonderland.* (The British Library.)

66.

at first, but she got quite used to it in a minute or two, and began talking to herself as usual : "well! there's half my plan done now! How puzzling all these changes are! I'm never sure what I'm going to be, from one minute to another! However, I've got to my right size again: the next thing is, to get into that beautiful garden — how is that to be done, I wonder?"

Just as she said this, she noticed that one of the trees had a doorway leading right into it. "That's very curious!" she thought, "but everything's curious today: I may as well go in." And in she went.

Once more she found herself in the long hall, and close to the little glass table: "now, I'll manage better this time" she said to herself, and began by taking the little golden key, and unlocking the door that led into the garden. Then she set to work eating the pieces of mushroom till she was about fifteen inches high: then she walked down the little passage: and then — she found herself at last in the beautiful garden, among the bright flowerbeds and the cool fountains.

CARTER, James Earl (Jimmy) b. 1924. 39th President of the USA, 1977–. Formerly Governor of Georgia. See also with US Presidents page 205.

CARTERET, John, 1st Earl Granville 1690–1763. British statesman. As virtual Head of Government twice in his career, his signature will also be found with British Prime Ministers page 68.

CARTIER, Jacques 1491–1557. French navigator. Discoverer of the St Lawrence river and explorer of the Canadian coast.

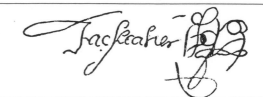

CARUSO, Enrico 1873–1921. Italian operatic tenor.
A signed example of Caruso's self-caricatures. (Author's Collection.)

CASALS, Pau (Pablo) 1876–1973. The great Spanish cellist. Also a conductor and composer.

CASANOVA, Giovanni Giacomo (or Jacopo) 1725–98. Italian adventurer, alchemist, sensualist and spy. His *Memoires* have made his name synonymous with a great lover of women.

CASEMENT, Roger (David) 1864–1916. Irish nationalist and British Consular official. Hanged by the British for treason, he is accepted in Eire as a martyr to his cause. His autograph is uncommon.

CASTELAR, Emilio 1832–99. Spanish statesman, orator and historian. A staunch republican.

CASTLEREAGH, Robert Stewart, Viscount 1769–1822. British statesman born in Ireland.
Castlereagh's signature can also be found as 'Londonderry'.

CASTRO (RUZ), Fidel b. 1927. Cuban revolutionary statesman and patriot. Overthrew the Batista regime in 1959 to become Prime Minister.

CATHERINE (II) THE GREAT 1729–96. Usurped the throne of her husband Peter III and became Empress of Russia, 1762. One of the most colourful of women rulers.
Signature in italic script and in Russian script on a court document. (Author's Collection.)

CATHERINE OF ARAGON, 1485–1536. First wife of **Henry VIII**. Daughter of the 'Catholic rulers' **Ferdinand** and **Isabella** of Spain.
See also under HENRY VIII.

CATHERINE de MEDICI(S), 1519–89. Queen of **Henry II** of France and mother of **Francis II, Charles IX** (during whose minority she was Regent of France) and **Henry III**.

CATHERINE (or KATHARINE) HOWARD, c. 1520–42. Fifth wife of **Henry VIII**. Beheaded on conviction for adultery.
See also under HENRY VIII.

CATHERINE PARR, 1512–48. Sixth wife of **Henry VIII**.
See also with HENRY VIII.

CAVENDISH, Henry 1731–1810. English chemist, physicist and natural philosopher. Made important chemical discoveries especially in relation to hydrogen, carbon dioxide, oxygen and nitric acid.

CAVOUR, Count Camillo Benso di 1810–61. Italian statesman. The 'founder' of the Italian state.
Part of ANS asking for a letter to be sent on to Baron Natale. (Author's Collection.)

CAWLEY, Evonne (*née* Goolagong) b. 1955. Australian tennis player. Wimbledon Ladies Singles Champion.

CELLINI, Benvenuto 1500–71. The great Italian goldsmith and sculptor. One of his most famous works was the golden salt-cellar of **Francis I** still preserved in the Vienna Museum. Part of an ALS to his one-time teacher **Michelangelo**. (The British Library.)

CERVANTES (SAAVEDRA), Miguel de 1547–1616. Spain's most famous novelist. The author of *Don Quixote*. It is interesting, autographically, that whereas a number of ALSs of Cervantes still exist, not a single page of the manuscript of *Don Quixote* has been preserved.
Variant examples of this very important autograph.

CETYWAYO, ?–1884. Zulu King who defeated the British at Isandhlwana (1879) but then lost the battle of Ulundi.
Cetywayo's autograph exists only in this form.

CÉZANNE, Paul 1839–1906. French impressionist painter.
Examples of his painting signature and of his usual holograph.

CHADWICK, Sir James b. 1891. British scientist. His discovery of the neutron brought him the Nobel Prize for Physics in 1935.

CHAGALL, Marc b. 1889. Russian painter. The first 'surrealist', a word said to have been coined by **Apollinaire** to describe Chagall's work.

CHALIAPIN, Fedor 1873–1938. Russian singer. One of the greatest bass singers of all time.
Signature and self-caricature. (Author's Collection.)

CHAMBERLAIN, (Arthur) Neville 1869–1940. British statesman.
See also with British Prime Ministers page 69.

CHAMPLAIN, Samuel de 1567–1635. French explorer in, and Governor of, Canada. Founder of Quebec.

CHAPLIN, Sir Charles (Spencer) b. 1889. 'Charlie Chaplin'. Film actor and director, famed for his tragi-comic roles as a baggy-trousered tramp-like figure.
PS. (Author's Collection.)

CHARDIN, Jean Baptiste Siméon 1699–1779. French painter. His country's greatest exponent of genre and still-life. An example of his signature on his paintings.

CHARLEMAGNE (or CHARLES I) 742–814. King of the Franks and Holy Roman Emperor. An excessively rare *signum*. The letters K.R.L.S. spell out his name in Latin leaving out the vowels. These letters are not holograph, but the small 'y' in the central diamond was inserted by Charlemagne himself. It represents the only known form of autograph of this great historical character.

CHARLES V, 1500–58. Holy Roman Emperor and King of Spain (as Charles I). One of the great royal figures of history. Examples of his signature as 'Charles' and 'Carolus' also D S 'Carolus' creating a Knight of Malta and according him a coat of arms. (Author's Collection.)

CHARLES I, 1600–49. King of Great Britain and Ireland. Succeeded 1625. Executed 1649.
For signature see also with British Sovereigns page 24.

CHARLES II, 1630–85. King of Great Britain and Ireland 1660 (restored)–1685.
For signature see also with British Sovereigns page 25.

CHARLES V, 1337–80. 'Charles the Wise', King of France 1364–80. He won back much of his country from the British.

CHARLES VI, 1368–1422. King of France 1380–1422. Usually known as 'Charles the Mad' because of his insanity from 1392. Lost the battle of Agincourt to **Henry V** of England.

CHARLES VII, 1403–61. King of France 1422–61. This was the somewhat ungrateful king whom **Joan of Arc** assisted in keeping his crown. Nonetheless, he ruled well thereafter.

CHARLES VIII, 1470–98. King of France 1483–98. Nicknamed 'the Affable'.

CHARLES IX, 1550–74. King of France 1560–74. Dominated by his mother **Catherine de Medici(s)**, he allowed the massacre of the Huguenots on St Bartholomew's Eve, 24 August 1572.

CHARLES XIV, 1763–1844. King of Sweden 1818–44. The Napoleonic Marshal Jean Baptiste Bernadotte.
For signature as Bernadotte see with Napoleonic Marshals at page 178.

CHARLES (PHILIP ARTHUR GEORGE), Prince b. 1948. Prince of Wales. Son of Queen **Elizabeth II**. Heir to the British throne.

CHARLTON, Robert 'Bobby' b. 1937. English footballer and football manager. In his international career, 1958–70, scored the record number of goals (49) for England.

CHARTERIS, Leslie b. 1907. British crime-story writer. Creator of 'The Saint'. Signature incorporating a 'pin-drawing' of his fictional hero.

CHATEAUBRIAND, François René, Vicomte de 1768–1848. French man of letters and statesman.

CHATTERTON, Thomas 1752–70. English poet. Poisoned himself after the rejection of his work.

Owing to his death at only eighteen years of age, this boy-poet's autograph is of the utmost rarity. An ANS of prophetic pathos. (The British Library.)

I must either live a Slave, a Servant; to have no Will of my own, no Sentiments of my own which I may freely declare as such; – or Die Perplexing Alternative! Thoˢ. Chatterton

CHAUCER, Geoffrey *c.* 1345–1400. English poet.
Signature and rare holograph document. (Public Record Office.)

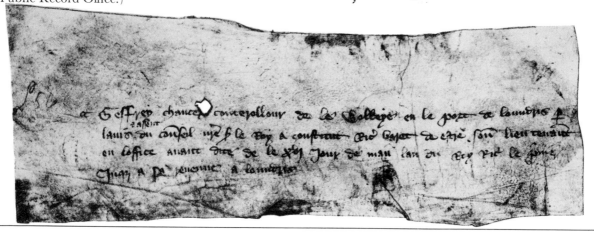

CHEKHOV (CHEKOV, CHEHOV or **TCHEKOV)**, Anton Pavlovich 1860–1904. Russian author. One of the most influential of his country's writers, his plays include *Uncle Vanya*, *The Cherry Orchard* and *Three Sisters*.
Variant autographs.

CHERUBINI, M Luigi C Z S 1760–1842. Italian composer. A highly successful director of the Paris Conservatoire of Music.

CHESTERTON, Gilbert Keith 1874–1936. English man of letters. Remembered for his witty verse, literary biographical studies and for his 'Father Brown' detective stories.

CHEVALIER, Maurice 1888–1972. French film actor and singer. Chevalier's success began as dancing partner to Mistinguett at the Folies Bergères before World War I, in which he distinguished himself and won both the Legion of Honour and the Croix de Guerre.
PS. (Author's Collection.)

CHEVREUIL. Michel Eugène 1786–1889. French chemist. Discovered margarine; also oleine and stearine. The centenarian scientist was known as 'le doyen des étudiants de France'.

CHIANG KAI-SHEK, 1887–1974. Chinese Generalissimo and Dictator. President of the Republic of China 1928–31. he was Head of the Executive 1935–45 and China's C-in-C against Japan. Withdrew from China to Taiwan (Formosa) where he was President from 1949 until his death.

CHICHESTER, Sir Francis 1901–72. British yachtsman and aviator. The first to circumnavigate the world solo with only one stop-over, 1966–7.

CHIFLEY, Joseph B 1885–1951. Australian Labour statesman. Prime Minister 1945–9.

C

CHOPIN, Frédéric 1810–49. Celebrated Franco-Polish composer. Signature on the printed music of his mazurkas (opus 30), with autograph authentication by fellow composer, Hector **Berlioz**. (Author's Collection.)

CHRISTIAN V, 1646–99. King of Denmark and Norway 1670–99.

CHRISTIE, Dame Agatha (Mary Clarissa) 1891–1976. Lady Mallowan. British best-selling detective novelist and playwright.

CHRISTINA, 1626–89. Queen of Sweden, 1632. An impetuous and extravagant ruler, she abdicated in 1654.

CHRISTOPHE, Henri 1767–1820. King of Haiti. A former negro slave who made himself President, and later, King after the defeat of the French and the overthrow of Dessalines.
Scarce letter to his son. (Author's Collection.)

CHURCHILL, Sir Winston (Leonard Spencer) 1874–1965. British Prime Minister. Early ALS and signed print of Frank O Salisbury's original painting (unsigned by Churchill) belonging to and reproduced by, permission of, the National Trust, Chartwell.

CLARENDON, Edward Hyde, 1st Earl of 1609–74. English statesman. Lord Chancellor and Head of Government under **Charles II**.

CLARK, Mark Wayne b. 1896. American soldier. C-in-C of the 5th Army in World War II.

CLAUDEL, Paul 1868–1955. French man of letters.
An example of his holograph.

CLEMENCEAU, Georges 1841–1929. French statesman known as 'the Tiger'. Twice Prime Minister, he presided over the Paris Peace Conference of 1919.

CLEMENT VII, 1478–1534. Pope 1523–34. Guilio de Medici. The papal ruler who supported **Francis I** against the Emperor **Charles V** and refused to sanction **Henry VIII**'s divorce from **Catherine of Aragon**.

CLEVELAND, (Stephen) Grover 1837–1908. Twenty-second and twenty-fourth President of the USA.
See also signature with US Presidents page 205.

CLIVE, Robert, Lord 1725–74. 'Clive of India'. British soldier and administrator in Bengal.

CNUT (KNUT or CANUTE) *c.* 994–1035. King of the English, Danes and Norwegians. The subject of the legend of his attempt to hold back the sea tide.
His *signum* (possibly not autograph but scribal) next his name (with other dignitaries) on a Grant to Aelfstan, Archbishop of Canterbury, of a grove near Hazelhurst; dated 1018. (British Library.)

COBBETT, William 1763–1835. Controversial English political writer and reformer. Twice lived in America where he wrote virulent criticisms under the pseudonym Peter Porcupine.

COCKCROFT, Sir John (Douglas) 1897–1967. English nuclear physicist. Nobel Prizewinner 1951.

COCKERELL, Sir Christopher Sydney b. 1910. British radio-engineer who invented the hovercraft.

COCTEAU, Jean 1889–1963. French poet and playwright.
Full signature and examples of the 'star' signature he frequently used.

CODY, William Frederick 1846–1917. 'Buffalo Bill'. American scout and showman. Care must be taken not to confuse Cody's signature with that of the Texan-English aviator, Samuel F Cody which resembles it.

COLBERT, Jean Baptiste 1619–83. French statesman, Chief Minister to **Louis XIV**.

COLERIDGE, Samuel Taylor 1772–1834. English poet. Unusual example from a Maltese Government document signed as 'Pub(lic) Sec(retary) to H.M.'s Civil Commission', a post he held for eighteen months, 1804–5.

COLERIDGE-TAYLOR, Samuel 1875–1921. English composer of *Hiawatha*, etc. Holograph musical extract.

COLETTE, Sidonie Gabrielle Claudine 1873–1954. French novelist. Pen name Colette.
A warm autograph note signed with a nickname 'La Rate'. (Author's Collection.)

COLIGNY, Gaspard de 1519–72. French admiral and Huguenot leader, murdered with the other victims of the St Bartholomew's Eve massacre, 24 August 1572. Signature as '(Sieu de) Chastillon'.

COLLINGWOOD, Cuthbert, Lord 1750–1810. English admiral. Took command at Trafalgar after **Nelson**'s death.

COLLINS, Michael 1890–1922. Irish Nationalist (Sinn Fein) leader. Assassinated. Collins' autograph – his signature in Gaelic is shown here – is comparatively rare.

COLMAN, Ronald 1891–1958. British film actor in Hollywood.

COLUMBUS, Christopher. In Italian Cristoforo Colombo. Spanish Cristóbal Colón 1451–1506. The discoverer of the New World.

There are several theories about the exact meaning of Columbus' cryptic signature, two examples of which, with a small extract from a holograph letter, are shown here. He is not known ever to have explained it himself. The Spanish archival authorities consider it to stand for, reading upwards – 'Cristoferens (the bearer of Christ): Cristo (X) Maria, Joseph: Sanctus'. The American S E Morison interprets it as 'Servant am I of the Most High Saviour, Christ, Son of Mary' with the name 'Christopher' in Greco-Latin style. A British theory (Beecher) is that it brings in a reference to his patrons **Ferdinand** and **Isabella** thus – 'Servidor Sus Altezas Sacras Jesu Maria Isabel Cristofero (Christ bearing).'

COMANECI, Nadia b. 1961. Romanian gymnast. At the age of fourteen she scored seven perfect scores of 10·00 and won three gold medals at the Olympic Games at Montreal, July 1976.

COMPTON, Spencer, Earl of Wilmington 1673–1743. English statesman. See also with British Prime Ministers page 68.

CONDORCET, M J Antoine Nicolas de Caritat, Marquis de 1743–94. French philosopher and mathematician.

CONGREVE, William 1670–1729. English dramatist and poet. His works include *Love for Love* and *The Way of the World*. Note that his signature is larger than his handwriting.

CONGREVE, Sir William 1772–1828. English soldier-scientist and inventor of the (Congreve) rocket.

CONNOLLY, Maureen (Catherine) 1934–69. 'Little Mo'. American tennis player. Three times Wimbledon and US tennis champion, she achieved her first Wimbledon title when aged seventeen.

CONRAD, Joseph 1857–1924. Polish-born English adventure novelist. Variant examples.

CONSTABLE, John 1776–1837. English landscape painter. One of the most desirable English art autographs.

CONSTANT (DE REBECQUE) (Henri) Benjamin 1767–1830. French writer and politician.

COOK, James 1728–79. 'Captain Cook', English navigator. Sailed round the world in the *Endeavour*. Explored and charted New Zealand, the Australian coast and the Pacific Isles. A rare autograph.
ALS of Cook concerning the fitting-out of *Endeavour*. (Public Record Office, London.)

COOLIDGE, Calvin 1872–1933. Thirtieth President of the USA.
See also with US Presidents page 205.

COOPER, James Fenimore 1789–1851. American novelist. Wrote *The Last of the Mohicans*.

COPERNICUS, Nicolaus 1473–1543. Polish-German astronomer. The 'founder' of modern astronomy as based on his principle of the earth's rotation on its axis round the sun. His usual autograph and signature in Greek.

COPLAND, Aaron b. 1900. American composer. His ballets *Appalachian Spring* and *Billy the Kid* are in the American folk-music tradition.

COQUELIN, (Benoît) Constant, called Coquelin aîné 1841–1909. French actor. Master of comedy.

CORBUSIER, Le, pseudonym of Charles E Jeanneret 1887–1965. Swiss architect. First achieved fame with his *Unité d'habitation* at Marseilles based on his scheme of town-planning, 'La ville radieuse'.

CORDAY (Marie) Charlotte 1768–93. French patriot and revolutionary. Revolted by the horrors of the 'Reign of Terror', she stabbed **Marat** in his bath for which she was guillotined. Signature from her passport.

CORDOBES, El (Manuel Benítez Pérez) b. 1936. 'The Man from Cordoba'. Spanish bullfighter, the highest paid in the history of this 'sport'.

CORNEILLE, Pierre 1606–84. French dramatist. Has been called the 'father' of both French tragedy and comedy.

CORNWALLIS, Charles, 1st Marquess of 1738–1805. British soldier and administrator. Forced to surrender at Yorktown when commanding the British Forces in the American War of Independence.

COROT, (Jean Baptiste) Camille 1796–1875. French painter. A man of great personal generosity he supported **Daumier** in his blindness and assisted similarly the widow of **Millet**.

CORTES, Hernan (do) 1485–1574. Spanish 'Conquistador'. Conquered Mexico and destroyed the Aztec empire.
A rare historical autograph.

CORTOT, Alfred 1877–1962. Swiss-born French pianist. He founded an internationally famous trio with Thibaud and **Casals**.

COURT, Margaret (née Smith). Australian tennis player. Has won all the world's major ladies' singles championships.

COUSIN, Victor 1792–1867. French philosopher. Despite his eminence, Cousin's autograph is neither scarce nor, inexplicably, greatly sought after.

COUSTEAU, Jacques Yves b. 1910. French underwater explorer and marine scientist. Inventor of the Aqualung. Captain of the oceanographic research ship *Calypso*.
PS. (Author's Collection.)

COWARD, Sir Noël 1899–1976. British playwright, actor and composer. 'The Master', celebrated for his witty comedies and musical plays.

COWPER, William 1731–1800. English poet. Cowper's scarce signature can sometimes be found on government papers as he was a Commissioner of Bankrupts for six years. It can also be easily confused with the very similar signature of his contemporary cousin of the same name who was Clerk of the Parliaments.

CRANACH, Lucas 1472–1553. German painter and engraver. Painted portraits of **Luther** and **Melanchthon**.

CRANMER, Thomas 1489–1556. Archbishop of Canterbury, burned at the stake. Variant signatures. Archbishops of Canterbury sign 'Cantuar' (Canterbury) after their Christian names. This can be shortened to 'Cant' or lengthened to 'Cantuarion'.

CRAWFORD, Joan 1908–77. American film actress. Born in Texas, she entered films in 1925 and rose rapidly to international stardom.

CRIPPEN, Hawley Harvey 1862–1910. Doctor Crippen, American-born wife murderer. The first criminal to be arrested by the use of radio-telegraphy.

CROCE, Benedetto 1866–1952. Italian historian, philosopher and critic. He was his country's Minister of Education, 1920–1.

CROCKETT, David 1786–1836. 'Davy' Crockett. American frontiersman, now a part of the legend of the Wild West.

CROMWELL, Oliver 1599–1658. Lord Protector of England. Cromwell's signature as 'Cromwell' is more scarce than as 'Oliver P(rotector)'. For both signatures see with British Sovereigns pages 24 and 25.

CROMWELL, Richard 1626–1712. Son and successor of Oliver Cromwell. Ruled for less than a year, and later took the name of Clarke. Rare signature as Protector. Also see with British Sovereigns page 25.

CROMWELL, Thomas *c.* 1485–1540. English statesman. 'Hammer of the Monks'. Succeeded his master, **Wolsey** as **Henry VIII**'s chief adviser. Executed.

CROOKES, Sir William 1832–1919. British scientist. Discovered thallium and the process of sodium amalgamation. Invented the radiometer.

CROSBY, Harry L, known as Bing b. 1904. American singer and film actor. Amongst other achievements he recorded the greatest seller of any gramophone record – 'White Christmas', by **Irving Berlin**.

CRUIKSHANK, George 1792–1878. Caricaturist and illustrator (of **Dickens**' novels, etc.).
An example of his extrovert signature. The author has another which is 7½ in long and 6 in high. Also a sketch signed characteristically 'GCk'. (Author's Collection.)

CUMBERLAND, William Augustus, Duke of 1721–65. English Prince and soldier. Second son of **George II**. His cruelties in crushing the Young Pretender's rebellion earned him the title of 'Butcher'.

CURIE, Irene Joliot- 1897–1956. French chemist. Daughter of **Pierre** and **Marie Curie**. Won Nobel Prize, 1935.

CURIE, Marie (*née* Sklodowska) 1867–1934. Polish-French physicist and chemist. Jointly with her husband, **Pierre** and Becquerel, she won a Nobel Prize for Physics in 1903 as a result of their work on radioactivity and their discovery of radium. In 1911 she received the Nobel Prize for Chemistry. She had discovered polonium in 1910. A rare and much sought-after autograph. The end portion of a scientific ALS. (Author's Collection.)

CURIE, Pierre 1859–1906. French physicist and chemist. Co-discoverer of radium with **Marie Curie**.
Pierre Curie's early death, as the result of being run over by a car in Paris, makes his autograph of great rarity. The short ALS herewith is of particular importance, dealing as it does with a negative test on some water thought to have been radioactive. (Author's Collection.)

CUSHMAN, Charlotte 1816–76. Distinguished American actress. Originally in opera, she first appeared in one of her principal roles as Lady Macbeth in 1835.

CUSTER, George Armstrong 1839–76. Courageous, if flamboyant, American soldier. Killed with his entire force by the Sioux Indians at Little Big Horn in Montana.

CUVIER, Baron Georges Léopold C F D 1769–1832. French naturalist and anatomist. Considered to be the founder of the sciences of comparative anatomy and palaeontology.

CYRANO de BERGERAC, Savinien 1619–55. French soldier, poet and writer, famed for his monstrous nose. The tragedy *Cyrano de Bergerac* by **Rostand** is based on him.

DAGUERRE, Louis J M 1789–1851. French pioneer of photography. Invented the daguerreotype process.

DAIMLER, Gottlieb 1834–1900. German inventor and automobile pioneer. PS. (Daimler-Benz Museum.)

DALAI LAMA, The (14th) b. 1934. Spiritual ruler of Tibet exiled on the occupation of his country by China, 1950.

DALI, Salvador b. 1904. Spanish painter. A prominent surrealist.

DALTON, John 1766–1844. English chemist. Propounded Dalton's Law of partial pressures of gases, etc. The first to describe colour blindness.
Variant signatures.

DAMIEN (de VEUSTER), Father Joseph 1840–89. Belgian missionary who lived and died (of leprosy) amongst the lepers of Hawaii.

DAMPIER, William 1652–1715. English buccaneer, circumnavigator and explorer. His name given to Dampier Archipelago and Strait.

D'ANNUNZIO, Prince Gabriele 1863–1938. Italian author, airman, soldier and patriot.

DANTON, Georges Jacques 1759–94. French Revolutionary leader. Guillotined after a struggle for power with **Robespierre**. Danton's autograph is becoming more scarce than that of his adversary.

DARLING, Grace 1815–42. English heroine of the sea. With her lighthouse-keeper father rescued the survivors of the *Forfarshire*, 1838. Owing to her short life, Grace Darling's autograph is scarce.

DARNLEY, Henry Stuart (Stewart), Lord 1545–67. Second husband – later murdered – of **Mary Queen of Scots**.
A rare Scottish historical autograph. Variant signatures, one as 'King'!

D'ARTAGNAN, Charles 1611–73. French soldier and swordsman. His fame is preserved in **Dumas'** *Three Musketeers*.

DARWIN, Charles (Robert) 1809–82. British naturalist famed for his theory of evolution, expounded in *The Origin of Species*. Darwin holographs are in very great demand. First and last pages of a 3 pp. ALS to Admiral Sir Bartholomew Sulivan who had served with him on the scientific voyage of the *Beagle*. Darwin refers to 'old Beaglers' and discusses scientific matters. (Author's Collection.)

DAUDET, Alphonse 1840–97. French writer of *Lettres de mon moulin* fame.
ALS refusing to write an article on Eton College having only seen it from the exterior and observed the 'rebounding games of its pupils'. (Author's Collection.)

DAUMIER, Honoré 1808–79. French painter and caricaturist.
Examples of his normal holograph and of his style of signing his work.

DAVID, Jacques Louis 1774–1825. French painter of the Revolution and the Napoleonic era.
See also **Robespierre** item at page 193.

DAVIS, Jefferson 1808–89. American statesman. President of the Confederate States during the American Civil War, 1861–5.

DAVIS, Joe b. 1901. British billiards and snooker player. Several times world champion in both games.

DAVOUT, Louis Nicolas, Prince of Eckmühl and Duke of Auerstädt 1770–1823. One of the most brilliant of **Napoleon**'s Marshals. See also with Napoleonic Marshals page 178.

DAVY, Sir Humphry 1778–1829. Prominent English chemist. Invented the miner's safety lamp and discovered potassium, sodium, calcium, magnesium and barium.

DAYAN, Moshe b. 1915. Israeli General. Held posts as Chief of Staff and Minister for Defence.

DEBUSSY, Claude Achille 1862–1918. Celebrated French composer. The example shown here is for a full ALS in which he discusses his 'madness' whilst orchestrating his 'Nocturnes'. (Author's Collection.) He died in a lunatic asylum.
Much in demand autographically.

D

DEFOE, Daniel 1660–1731. English novelist and man of letters. Famed for the classic novel *Robinson Crusoe*.

DEGAS, (H G) Edgar 1834–1917. French impressionist painter.
Examples of his usual holograph and of the signature he used on his paintings.

DE GAULLE, Charles A J M 1890–1970. French General, patriot and first President of the Fifth Republic.

DE HAVILLAND, Sir Geoffrey 1882–1965. British pioneer airman and aircraft designer. Produced the famous Tiger Moth and Mosquito 'planes.

DELACROIX, (F V), Eugène 1798–1863. Leading French romantic and historical painter.
Handwriting and variant signatures.

DELAREY, Jacobus Hercules 1847–1914. The most brilliant of the Boer Generals in guerrilla fighting in the South African War. A none too common South African autograph.

DELIBES, Léo 1836–91. French composer of light opera and ballet – in particular *Coppélia*.

DELIUS, Frederick 1862–1934. British composer, blind from 1924.

DEMPSEY, William H ('Jack') b. 1895. American boxer. Heavyweight champion of the world, 1919–26. One of the all-time greats of boxing history.

DE QUINCEY, Thomas 1785–1859. English writer, of the classic, *Confessions of an Opium Eater*, etc. End portion of a complete letter to a professor to whom he owes money for tuition of his daughter. De Quincey was frequently in financial trouble! (Author's Collection.)

DERBY, Edward (G S) Stanley, 14th Earl of 1799–1869. British statesman and Premier.
See also with British Prime Ministers page 69.

DESCARTES, René 1596–1650. French philosopher, scientist and mathematician. Founder of cartesianism and analytical geometry.

DESMOULINS, Camille 1760–94. French Revolutionary and journalist. Guillotined.

DE VALERA, Eamon 1882–1975. Irish statesman and patriot. After the early stormy years of revolution became Prime Minister and President of Eire.

D

DEVONSHIRE, William Cavendish, 4th Duke of 1720–64. Prime Minister 1756–7. Devonshire's signature, the most scarce of all British Prime Ministers' autographs, is also shown at page 68.

DEVONSHIRE, Victor C W Cavendish, 9th Duke of 1868–1938. Governor-General of Canada 1916–21.
See also Introduction.

DIAGHILEV, Sergei P 1872–1929. Russian impresario, who founded the Ballets Russes to which both **Nijinsky** and **Pavlova** belonged. An important and uncommon ballet autograph.

DIAZ, (J de la Cruz) Porfirio 1830–1915. Mexican soldier and statesman. President of Mexico in two spells covering 30 years.

DIAZ (de VIVAR or BIVAR), Rodrigo. 'EL CID' 1043–99. The almost legendary Spanish warrior hero, immortalised in epic poems and dramas. Nicknamed 'El Cid' from the Moorish 'Sidi' (My Lord). Also called 'Campeador' (Champion).
Excessively rare autograph of El Cid in Latin. The holograph section, from the word 'ego', can be translated as 'I Rodrigo with my wife, confirm what is written above'.

DICKENS, Charles 1812–70. The great English novelist of *Pickwick Papers*, *Oliver Twist*, *David Copperfield*, etc. ALS concerning *A Christmas Carol*. (Author's Collection.)

DICKINSON, Emily 1830–86. American poetess.

DIDEROT, Denis 1713–84. French philosopher and encyclopaedist. An important French literary autograph.

DIESEL, Rudolph 1858–1913. German mechanical engineer. Invented the diesel (internal combustion) engine. Signatures varying with increasing age.

(1876) (1890) (1898) (1912)

DIETRICH, Marlene b. 1904. German film actress, the epitome of 'glamour'. Her fame began with *The Blue Angel*, after which she went to Hollywood appearing in a succession of major films. Also distinguished in cabaret performances.

DISNEY, Walt(er) 1901–66. American artist and film producer, in particular of animated cartoons. His studio signature.

DISRAELI, Benjamin, Earl of Beaconsfield 1804–81. Statesman and novelist.
See also with British Prime Ministers page 69.

DOLFUSS, Engelbert 1892–1934. Austrian statesman and Chancellor. Murdered by Austrian Nazi rebels.
A scarce autograph.

DÖNITZ (or DOENITZ) Karl b. 1891. German Grand-Admiral who succeeded **Hitler** as Führer and ordered the surrender of Germany in 1945.

D

DONIZETTI, Gaetano 1797–1848. Italian composer.
ALS concerning a cantata. (Author's Collection.)

DONNE, John 1572–1631. Major English metaphysical poet.

DORÉ, Gustave 1833–83. French painter and illustrator particularly of the classics, such as the works of Dante, **Cervantes**, **Tennyson**, **Balzac** and **Rabelais**.

DORIA, Andrea *c*. 1466–1560. Genoese admiral and patriot. 'The Liberator of Genoa'. He fought for **Francis I** and then for the **Emperor Charles V**. He established the separate state of Genoa.

DOSTOEVSKI (or DOSTOYEVSKI) Fyodor Michailovich 1821–81. Russian novelist. His masterpiece is *Crime and Punishment*.

DOUGLAS-HOME, Sir Alec F, Baron Home b. 1903. British statesman. See also with British Prime Ministers page 69.

DOYLE, Sir Arthur Conan 1859–1930. English novelist. Creator of the detective Sherlock Holmes.

DRAKE, Sir Francis *c.* 1540–96. English Admiral and navigator. The greatest of the Elizabethan seamen, he was the first Englishman to circumnavigate the world. Variant signatures. Also part ALS about the defeat of the Spanish Armada. (Public Record Office, London.)

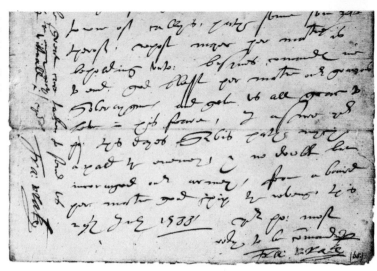

DREISER, Theodore 1871–1945. American writer. His most distinguished work is probably *An American Tragedy*, 1925.

DREYFUS, Alfred 1859–1935. French Army officer wrongly convicted of treason and sent to Devil's Island. Largely by the efforts of **Zola** he was acquitted and reinstated.

DRYDEN, John 1631–1700. Celebrated English poet. Dryden's autograph is rare.

DU BARRY, Marie, Comtesse de 1741–93. Influential favourite of **Louis XV**. She was guillotined in the French Revolution.

DUBCEK, Alexander b. 1921. Czechoslovak Communist statesman and patriot. As First Secretary in 1968, he attempted liberal reforms, which brought about his fall. A scarce item.

DUKAS, Paul 1865–1935. French composer known in particular for his symphonic poem *The Sorcerer's Apprentice*.

DUKE, Geoff(rey) b. 1923. British world champion racing motor cyclist. Retired to the Isle of Man where he had achieved so many of his successes.

DUMAS, Alexandre (*père*) 1802–70. French novelist. Author of *The Three Musketeers*, *The Count of Monte Cristo*, etc.

DUMAS, Alexandre (*fils*) 1824–95. Son of the foregoing. French novelist, dramatist and essayist.
Autograph quotation from one of his works.
(Author's Collection.)

DUNLOP, John Boyd 1840–1921. Scottish inventor of the pneumatic tyre. He had previously been a successful veterinary surgeon.

DÜRER, Albrecht 1471–1528. Germany's most famous artist-engraver.
Examples of his normal autograph and of one of the several devices with which he signed his work.

DURRELL, Lawrence G b. 1912. British novelist and poet. His works include *Prospero's Cell* and *Bitter Lemons*.

DUSE, Eleonora 1859–1924. Italian actress, one of the greatest of all time.

DVOŘÁK, Antonin 1841–1904. Czech composer. Much of his music was influenced by his friendship with **Brahms**.

EARHART, Amelia 1898–1937. American pioneer aviatrix. First woman to fly across the Atlantic, 1928. Lost on Pacific flight.

EDDY, Mary Baker 1821–1910. Founder of Christian Science and of its church.

EDEN, Sir (R) Anthony, Earl of Avon 1897–1977. British Conservative statesman. See also with British Prime Ministers page 69.

EDISON, Thomas Alva 1847–1931. American inventor. Patented over 1000 inventions, including the phonograph (gramophone), megaphone, microphone, kinetoscope and incandescent lighting.

EDWARD III, 1312–77. King of England 1327–77. Part of a DS (1350), the final line being attributed to the king. The oldest surviving example of a sovereign's autograph. (Public Record Office, London.)

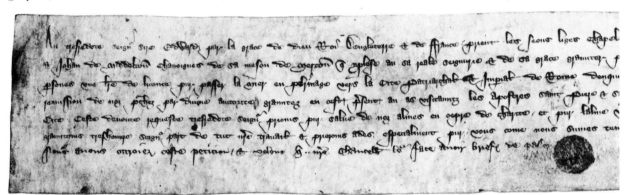

EDWARD IV, 1442–83. King of England 1461–83.
Rare signature as Earl of March. For monarchical signature see page 24.

EDWARD V, 1470–83. King of England for approximately 75 days 1483 until his murder in the Tower of London.
Excessively rare signature. See also British Sovereigns page 24.

EDWARD VI, 1537–53. King of England 1547–53. Son of **Henry VIII** and **Jane Seymour**.
A very rare signature. See also with British Sovereigns page 24.

British Prime Ministers

The title of Prime Minister was officially adopted in 1905 but it is accepted that the office, synonymous with that of First Lord of the Treasury, dates from Walpole's ministry in 1721. Names, dates of holding office and autographic comments only will be found on these pages. For biographical details see under individual entries in the main text.

The Prime Ministers are:

1. Sir Robert Walpole. 1721–42. He signed 'Orford' from 1742.
2. Spencer Compton. 1742–3. Signatures as 'Compton' and as Earl of Wilmington, from 1728.
3. Henry Pelham. 1743–54, with a short break in February 1746.
4. Earl of Bath, W Pulteney. Not generally recognised as a Prime Minister but held the seals 10–12 February 1746.
5. John, Lord Carteret. Held seals of office for four days in February 1746.
6. Duke of Newcastle. 1754–6, 1757–62.
7. 4th Duke of Devonshire. 1756–7. His autograph is the most scarce of the British Premiers.
8. 2nd Earl Waldegrave. Not universally accepted as a Prime Minister, he held office for four days, 8–12 June 1757.
9. Earl of Bute. 1762–3. His autograph is none too common.
10. George Grenville. 1763–5.
11. Marquis of Rockingham. 1765–6, 1782.
12. William Pitt, the Elder. 1766–7. He signed 'Chatham' after 1766.
13. Duke of Grafton. 1767–70.
14. Frederick, Lord North. 1770–82.
15. Earl of Shelburne. 1782–3.
16. Duke of Portland. 1783, 1807–9.
17. William Pitt, the Younger. 1783–1801, 1804–6.
18. Henry Addington, Viscount Sidmouth. 1801–4. Signed 'Sidmouth' from 1805.
19. Lord Grenville. 1806–7.
20. Spencer Perceval. 1809–12.
21. 2nd Earl of Liverpool. 1812–27. He signed 'Hawkesbury' until 1808.
22. George Canning. April–September, 1827.
23. Viscount Goderich. 1827–8. He signed 'Ripon' after 1833.
24. Duke of Wellington. 1828–30.
25. 2nd Earl Grey. 1830–4.
26. Viscount Melbourne. 1834, 1835–41.
27. Sir Robert Peel. 1834–5, 1841–6. Care must be taken in identifying his autograph as his son's was very similar.

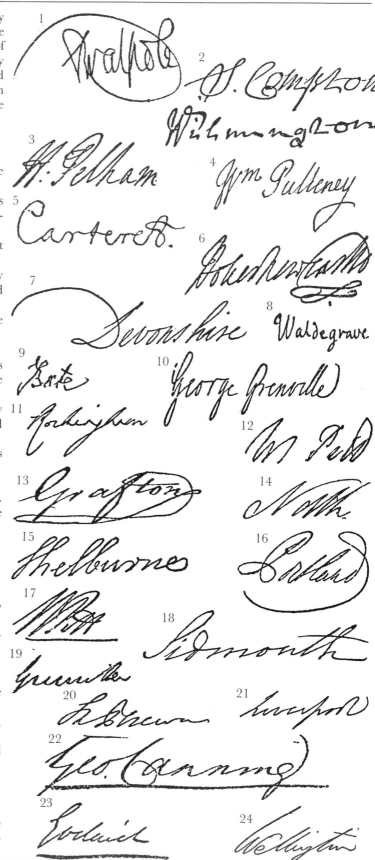

28. Lord John, Earl Russell. 1846–52, 1865–6.
29. 14th Earl of Derby. 1852, 1858–9, 1866–8. He signed 'Stanley' 1844–51.
30. 4th Earl of Aberdeen. 1852–5.
31. 2nd Viscount Palmerston. 1855–8, 1859–65.
32. Benjamin Disraeli. 1868, 1874–80. He often signed only 'D' and from 1876 he signed 'Beaconsfield'.
33. W E Gladstone. 1868–74, 1880–5, 1886, 1892–4.
34. 3rd Marquis of Salisbury. 1885–6, 1886–92, 1895–1902.
35. 5th Earl of Rosebery. 1894–5. Often signed with his initial only.
36. A J Balfour. 1902–5.
37. Sir Henry Campbell-Bannerman. 1905–8.
38. H H Asquith. 1908–15, 1915–16.
39. David Lloyd George. 1916–22.
40. Andrew Bonar Law. 1922–3.
41. Stanley Baldwin. 1923–4, 1924–9, 1935–7. Signed 'Baldwin of Bewdley' after 1937.
42. J Ramsay MacDonald. 1924, 1929–31, 1931–5.
43. A Neville Chamberlain. 1937–40.
44. Sir Winston Churchill. 1940–5, 1945, 1951–5. His shortened signature used frequently when out of office in the 1930s and in old age: and a more typical signature.
45. C R Atlee. 1945–51.
46. Sir Anthony Eden. 1955–7. Signed 'Avon' after 1957.
47. Harold Macmillan. 1957–63.
48. Sir Alec Douglas-Home. 1963–4. He signed 'Home' until disclaiming his Earldom in 1963 and again on becoming a life Baron in 1976.
49 J Harold (now Sir Harold) Wilson. 1964–6, 1966–70, 1974, 1974–6.
50. Edward R. G. Heath. 1970–4.
51. James Callaghan. 1976–.

EDWARD VII, 1841–1910. King of Great Britain and Ireland and Emperor of India, 1901–10. 'The Peacemaker'.
See also British Sovereigns page 25.

EDWARD VIII, 1894–1972. King of Great Britain and Emperor of India, January–December 1936. Son of **George V**, he was a very popular Prince of Wales until his accession and subsequent abdication as a result of the constitutional crisis caused by his proposed marriage to Mrs Simpson. Thereafter he was created Duke of Windsor.
For variant signatures see with British Sovereigns page 25.

EDWARD THE BLACK PRINCE, 1330–76. Warrior prince, so called for his black armour. Eldest son of **Edward III**. Unique signature 'De par Hotnout Ich Dene'.

EIFFEL, Gustave 1832–1923. French engineer who built the Eiffel Tower in Paris.

EINSTEIN, Albert 1879–1955. German-born American mathematical physicist. Responsible for the theory of relativity, etc. Won Nobel Prize, 1921. A greatly sought-after autograph.

EISENHOWER, Dwight David 1890–1969. American General and Thirty-fourth President of the USA.
See also with US Presidents page 205.

ELGAR, Sir Edward 1857–1934. British composer famed for the *Pomp and Circumstance* marches, the oratorio, *Dream of Gerontius*, and other works. Autograph musical extract from his *Sea Pictures*. (Author's Collection.)

'ELIOT, George', pseudonym of Marian Evans 1819–80. English novelist, famed for *Adam Bede*, *The Mill on the Floss*, etc. Examples of her rare pseudonym signature and her autograph as M(arian) E(vans) Lewes. The latter, taken from G H Lewes, the journalist with whom she lived for 24 years, is the most commonly found form of her signature.

ELIOT, T(homas) S(tearns) 1888–1965. American-born British poet, critic and dramatist. Won Nobel Prize for Literature, 1948.

ELIZABETH I, 1533–1603. Queen of England 1558–1603. Daughter of **Henry VIII** and **Anne Boleyn**. An able and determined ruler whose reign saw the beginnings of the British Empire through the expeditions of the great English navigators, **Drake**, **Raleigh**, **Hawkins**, **Frobisher** and others. It also saw the growth of commerce and the encouragement of the arts.
See also with British Sovereigns page 24.

ELIZABETH II, b. 1926. Queen of the United Kingdom and Head of the Commonwealth. Daughter of **George VI**. PS with the Duke of Edinburgh (Sir Brian Marwich). Photo by Anthony Buckley.
See also with British Sovereigns page 25.

ELIZABETH OF BOHEMIA, 1596–1662. Queen of Bohemia. Daughter of **James I** of England. Called 'The Queen of Hearts'.

EMERSON, Ralph Waldo 1803–82. American man of letters. Particularly distinguished as an essayist, he was also successful as a poet.

ENGELS, Friedrich 1820–95. German Socialist philosopher. Collaborated with **Karl Marx** in the *Communist Manifesto*, 1847.

EPSTEIN, Sir Jacob 1880–1959. Powerful and controversial American-born British sculptor.

ERASMUS, Desiderius 1466–1536. Eminent Dutch humanist scholar, religious reformer and philosopher.
Varying forms of his rare and important autograph.

ESPARTERO, Baldomero 1792–1879. Prince of Vergara. Spanish soldier and statesman. At one time his name was put forward for the Spanish throne.

ESSEX, Robert Devereux, 2nd Earl of 1566–1601. English nobleman. Favourite of **Elizabeth I**. Executed for treason.

EUCKEN, Rudolf Christoph 1846–1926. German activist philosopher. Won Nobel Prize for literature, 1908.

EUGENE OF SAVOY, 1663–1736. Austrian Prince and General. Joined with **Marlborough** in his great victories. An example of his signature in Italian. He also signed in German and French.

EVELYN, John 1620–1706. English diarist and writer on a wide variety of subjects. As a diarist, second only to **Pepys**.

FAIRBANKS, Douglas (Senior) 1883–1939. American film actor. The epitome of the swashbuckling hero type of the silent films.

FAISAL (BIN ABDUL AZIZ), 1904–75. King of Saudi Arabia 1964–75. Assassinated.

FALLA, Manuel de 1876–1946. Spanish composer. His ballet, *The Three-Cornered Hat,* was a particular success.

FANGIO (y CIA), Juan Manuel b. 1911. Argentine racing motorist. Five times world champion.

FANTIN-LATOUR, Ignace H J T 1836–1904. French painter.
An example of his painting signature.

FARADAY, Michael 1791–1867. English chemist and physicist. Regarded as the founder of electrochemistry.

FARMAN, Henri 1874–1858. French pioneer aviator. With brother Maurice, introduced the biplane.

F

FAROUK, 1920–65. King of Egypt 1937–52. Son of **Fouad**, he was forced to abdicate by a military *coup d'état*.

FARRAGUT, David G 1801–70. American Admiral. Distinguished himself in the Civil War.

FAULKNER (or **FALKNER**), William Harrison 1897–1962. American author. Won Nobel Prize for Literature, 1949.

FAURÉ, Gabriel U 1845–1924. French composer.
Holograph signed extract from a sonata for violin and piano. (Author's Collection.)

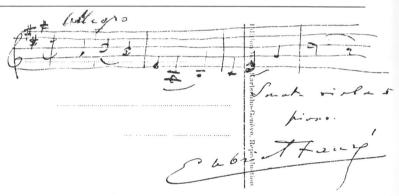

FAWKES, Guy 1570–1606. English conspirator. Hanged for his attempt to blow up King **James I** and Parliament. His second confession. End page thereof, with the names of the other principal conspirators. Signed 'Guido Fawkes' and countersigned by Sir Edward Coke, the Attorney General and Sir William Waad, the Constable of the Tower of London, 17 November 1605. (Public Record Office, London.)

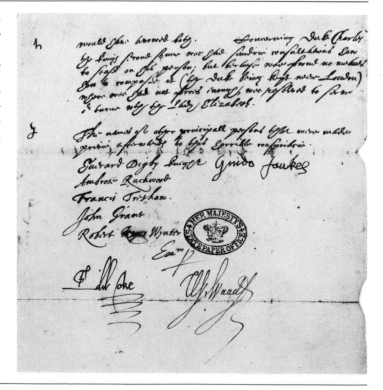

FÉNELON, François de Salignac de la Mothe 1651–1715. French theologian and writer.
Signature as Archbishop of Cambrai.

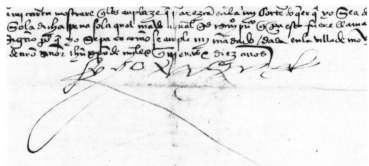

FERDINAND V, 'The Catholic', 1452–1516. King of Castile, Aragon and Sicily. Ruled with his queen, **Isabella** what was the forerunner of the present state of Spain. They were the patrons of **Columbus**. Ferdinand's autograph is much more rare that that of his wife.
Signature (from a DS) as 'Yo el Rey'.

FERMI, Enrico 1901–54. Italian-American physicist. Awarded Nobel Physics Prize 1938 for work on radioactive substances by neutron bombardment. Also produced the first nuclear reactor. A rare autograph.

FEUCHTWANGER, Lion 1889–1958. German Jewish writer famed for his classic *Jud Süss*.

FIELDING, Henry 1707–54. English author and satirist particularly famous for his novel *Tom Jones*. Another branch of Fielding's activities is shown by this letter to the Lord Chancellor sending a draft Bill to prevent Street Roberries. With his brother, Sir John Fielding, the blind Magistrate, he established the precursors of the modern police force, the Bow Street Runners. ALS dated Bow Street, 21 July 1749 (the year of Fielding's famous novel *Tom Jones*). (The British Library.)

FILLMORE, Millard 1800–74. Thirteenth President of the USA.
See signature with US Presidents page 204.

FITZGERALD, F. Scott (K) 1896–1940. American novelist of *The Great Gatsby*, etc. Recently an upsurge of nostalgic interest in 'the Twenties' has led to a considerable demand for Scott Fitzgerald's autograph.

FLAMMARION, Camille 1842–1925. French astronomer. Opened an observatory at Juvisy.

FLAMSTEED, John 1646–1719. English astronomer. The first Astronomer-Royal. His work assisted Newton with his lunar theory.

FLAUBERT, Gustave 1821–80. French novelist. *Madame Bovary* was his masterpiece.

FLAXMAN, John 1755–1826. English sculptor. He designed for **Wedgwood** as well as other work.

FLEMING, Sir Alexander 1881–1955. Scottish bacteriologist. Discovered penicillin in 1928 and in 1945 shared a Nobel Prize with Chain and **Florey** for its development.

FLEMING, Sir (J) Ambrose 1849–1945. British electrical engineer and physicist. Invented the thermionic valve.

FLEMING, Ian (L) 1908–64. British author. The creator of 'James Bond' about whose exploits several films have been made.

FLEURY, André Hercule de 1653–1743.
Cardinal and Chief Minister of **Louis XV**.

FLOREY, Howard W, Lord 1898–1968.
Australian-born British pathologist. Shared
the Nobel Prize for Medicine, 1945 with
Alexander Fleming and Chain for work on
penicillin.

FOCH, Ferdinand 1851–1929. French
Marshal. Successful generalissimo of the
Allied Armies in World War I.

FOKINE, Michel 1880–1942. Russian
dancer and choreographer. The creator of
modern ballet.

FONTEYN (-ARIAS), Dame Margot b.
1919. English prima ballerina.

FORD, Gerald b. 1913. Thirty-eighth
President of the USA.
See also with US Presidents page 205.

FORD, Henry 1863–1947. American pioneer automobile designer and manufacturer. A major philanthropist.

FORSTER, E(dward) M(organ) 1879–
1970. English author of the classic
A Passage to India, etc.

FOUAD (or **FUAD**), 1868–1936. Sultan of Egypt 1917–1922. King 1922–1936.

FOUCHÉ, Joseph, Duke of Otranto 1763–1820. Napoleon's police minister and master spy.

FOX, Charles James 1749–1806. English Liberal statesman and orator. A desirable British political autograph.

FRAGONARD, Jean-Honoré 1732–1806. French genre painter of contemporary court life and landscapes.
Fragonard's autograph is very rare.

FRANCE, Anatole, pseudonym of Anatole François Thibault 1844–1924. French writer.
Initialled ANS concerning a book by **Montesquieu**. (Author's Collection.)

FRANCIS I, 1494–1547. King of France 1515–47. Like his contemporary, **Henry VIII**, he was cruel and licentious, yet patronised the arts.

DS 1540 setting out the pay of the postilions of the Royal train. (Author's Collection.)

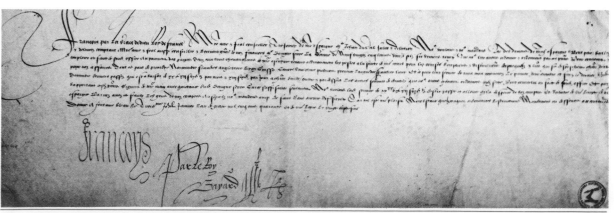

FRANCIS II, 1544–60. King of France 1559–60. First husband of **Mary Queen of Scots**.
Owing to his short life and one-year reign, his autograph is scarce.

FRANCIS JOSEPH (or **FRANZ JOSEPH**), 1830–1916. Austro-Hungarian emperor.

FRANCIS OF ASSISI, Saint (Giovanni Bernadone) 1182–1226. Italian friar and preacher who founded the Franciscan Order. Fabled for his love of animals. Canonised 1228.
This example of his handwriting is taken from *Handwriting Tells* by Nadya Olyanova by kind permission of the publishers, Peter Owen of London.

FRANCIS DE BORJA, Saint 1510–72. Duke of Gandia. A founder-member with his friend, Saint **Ignatius Loyala**, of the Jesuits. A Spaniard himself and of a very different character, he was a cousin of the notorious Italian Borgias.
His scarce signature reads 'Fran(cis)co pecador' – 'Francis the sinner'.

FRANCIS OF SALES, Saint 1567–1622. French Jesuit ecclesiastic and preacher. With Sainte Jeanne de Chantal, founded the Order of Sisters of the Visitation. Signature as Bishop (Évêque) of Geneva.

FRANCIS XAVIER, Saint (Francisco Javier) 1506–52. Spanish missionary. 'The Apostle of the Indies'. Founded with **Saint Ignatius Loyola** the Society of Jesus (Jesuits). Canonised 1622.

FRANCK, César (A) 1822–90. Belgian-French composer and organist.
ALS asking the organist of St Philippe's if he may take his place to play at the wedding of one of his pupils. (Author's Collection.)

FRANCO (BAHAMONDE), Francisco 1892–1975. Generalissimo and Head of State of Spain 1936–75.

FRANKLIN, Benjamin 1706–90. American statesman, scientist and philosopher. A highly sought-after autograph. See also frontispiece.

FRANKLIN, Sir John 1786–1847. British Arctic explorer and navigator. Lost in search for the Northwest Passage.

FRASER, Peter 1884–1950. Prime Minister of New Zealand 1940–49.

FREDERICK I BARBAROSSA, *c.* 1122–90. 'Redbeard', the warrior Emperor of the Holy Roman Empire, 1152–90, who led the Third Crusade.
The *signum* on the right of the titular description is in the Emperor's own holograph and is of extreme rarity. Both are from a document dated 1166 sold at auction by Stargardt of Marburg, Germany.

FREDERICK II, 'The Great', 1712–86.
King of Prussia. A writer, patron of the arts
and skilful administrator.

FREDERICK WILLIAM I, 1688–1740.
King of Prussia 1713–40. 'The Soldier
King'.
An unusual form of his signature in French
'Fr. Guillaume'.

FREDERICK WILLIAM III, 1770–1840.
King of Prussia 1797–1840. Opponent of
Napoleon.

FRENCH, Sir John, Earl of Ypres
1852–1925. British Field-Marshal. C-in-C in
France 1914–15.

FREUD, Sigmund 1856–1939. Austrian
psychiatrist. Founder of psychoanalysis.
Autographically, Freud is very much in
demand and becoming somewhat scarce.
An ANS to David Davies of London
thanking him for sending Freud his book
The Problem of the Twentieth Century. Vienna,
11 July 1933. (Author's Collection.)

FROBISHER, Sir Martin *c.* 1535–94.
English navigator and naval commander.

FROEBEL, Friedrich W A 1782–1852.
German educationalist. Founder of the
kindergarten system.

FROST, Robert (Lee) 1874–1963. American lyric poet. Expressed, in verse, the
character of New England.

FRY, Elizabeth 1780–1845. English Quaker prison reformer and philanthropist.

FUCHS, Sir Vivian E b. 1908. British Antarctic explorer and scientist. Led the first overland crossing of the Antarctic, 1957–8.

FUGGER, Count Anton 1493–1560. One of the great German commercial and financial house founded by his grandfather, Jakob.

FULTON, Robert 1765–1815. American inventor and engineer. Built the first successful American steamboat, *Clermont*, 1807.

FURTWÄNGLER, Wilhelm 1886–1954. German orchestral conductor.

GABLE, Clark 1901–60. American film actor.

GAGARIN, Yuri 1934–68. Russian cosmonaut. The first man to travel in space, he circuited the earth in Vostok space satellite, 1961. Killed in a plane accident.

His early death, combined with the dearth of modern Russian autograph material, makes Gagarin's autograph scarce but it will eventually be exceedingly rare. Signature and PS. (Author's Collection.)

GAINSBOROUGH, Thomas 1727–88. The great English landscape and portrait painter.

G

GALILEO (GALILEI), Galileo 1564–1642. The famed Italian astronomer, mathematician and physicist. Constructed the first astronomical telescope.
ALS to **Michaelangelo**. (The British Library.)

GALLI-CURCI, Amelita 1882–1963. Italian soprano prima donna.

GALSWORTHY, John 1867–1933. British author of *The Forsyte Saga*, etc. Won Nobel Prize for Literature, 1932.

GALTON, Sir Francis 1822–1911. British scientist and explorer. Founder of the science of eugenics. Pioneer of fingerprint identification.

GALVANI, Luigi 1737–98. Italian physiologist. Studied animal electricity. 'Galvanising' derives from his name.

GAMA, Vasco da *c.* 1469–1525. Celebrated Portuguese navigator. Rounded the Cape of Good Hope to India. Became Governor of Portuguese India.
Part ALS signed as Count of Vidigueira. (Lisbon Geographical Society Museum.)

GANDHI, Indira b. 1917. Prime Minister of India 1966–77. Daughter of **Nehru**.

GANDHI, Mohandas Karamchand 1869–1948. Mahatma ('great-souled') Gandhi. Indian patriot, nationalist and religious leader. The apostle of passive resistance, he strove most of his life for Indian independence. Killed by a Hindu fanatic.
An early example of Gandhi's highly sought-after autograph.

GARBO, Greta b. 1905. Swedish-American film actress famed for her unusual beauty as much as for her acting. Owing to her expressed wish to be 'left alone', Greta Garbo's autograph is rare.
PS. (Author's Collection.)

GARCIA, Manuel 1805–1906. Spanish centenarian singer and teacher. Inventor of the laryngoscope.

GARCIA LORCA, Federigo 1899–1936. Spanish poet and playwright. He was killed in the Spanish Civil War.

GARDNER, Erle Stanley 1889–1970. American detective-story writer. Creator of 'Perry Mason'. Probably the world's fastest-working novelist, he dictated up to 10,000 words a day.

GARFIELD, James Abram 1831–81. Twentieth President of the USA. Assassinated.
See also US Presidents page 205.

GARIBALDI, Giuseppe 1807–82. Italian patriot and soldier. With **Cavour** and **Mazzini** one of the founders of the state of Italy.

GARRICK, David 1717–79. Actor-manager and dramatist. One of the greatest names of the English theatre.

GASKELL, Elizabeth Cleghorn 1810–65. English novelist. Her most famous work was *Cranford*.

GAUGUIN, (E H) Paul 1848–1903. French painter. Gauguin's fairly scarce autograph changed considerably at different periods of his life.
Variant examples.

GAUTIER, Théophile 1811–72. French man of letters.

GAY-LUSSAC, Joseph Louis 1778–1850. French chemist. Discovered the element Boron.

GEORGE I, 1660–1727. King of Great Britain and Ireland 1714–27. Content to leave administration to his ministers, thus creating the cabinet system of government.
See also with British Sovereigns page 25.

GEORGE II, 1683–1760. King of Great Britain and Ireland 1727–60. The last British king to lead his troops in battle, at Dettingen, 1743.
See also with British Sovereigns page 25.

GEORGE III, 1738–1820. King of Great Britain and Ireland 1760–1820. Although on the whole a popular ruler, the American colonies were lost during his reign and recurring insanity made necessary the regency of his son, later **George IV**. Variant signatures.
See signature with British Monarchs page 25.

GEORGE IV, 1762–1830. King of Great Britain and Ireland 1820–30. Acted as Prince Regent for his father, **George III**, 1811–20.
See also with British Sovereigns page 25.

GEORGE V, 1865–1936. King of the United Kingdom and Emperor of India 1910–36.
See also with British Sovereigns page 25.

GEORGE VI, 1895–1952. King of the United Kingdom 1936–52, after the abdication of his brother **Edward VIII**.
See also with British Sovereigns page 25.

GERMAN, Sir Edward 1862–1936. British composer.
Holograph musical extract from *Richard III*. (Author's Collection.)

GERONIMO, 1829–1909. Chief of the American Indian Apache tribe, his original name was Goyathlay.
This example shows the only form of his signature.

GERSHWIN, George 1898–1937. American composer of *Rhapsody in Blue*, *Porgy and Bess*, etc.
Autograph shown with that of his brother Ira, his lyricist.

GETTY, J Paul 1892–1976. American oil billionaire.

GIBBON, Edward 1737–94. English historian famed for his *Decline and Fall of the Roman Empire*.

GIBBONS, Grinling 1648–1721. English sculptor and woodcarver. His work decorates several **Wren** churches.
An uncommon autograph.

GIDE, André (P G) 1869–1951. French writer.
An example of his holograph.

GIGLI, Beniamino 1890–1957. Italian tenor.

GILBERT (or GYLBERT), Sir Humphrey 1537–83. British navigator. Took possession of Newfoundland for **Elizabeth I** in 1583.

GILBERT, Sir William Schwenk 1836–1911. English playwright and lyricist. Librettist of the 'Gilbert and Sullivan' operas. Signature and part ALS concerning Sullivan. (Richmond Borough Council.)

GISCARD D'ESTAING, V b. 1926. President of France 1974.
ANS: by courtesy of the French Embassy, London.

GISSING, George Robert 1857–1903. English novelist.
Gissing's autograph is uncommon.

GLADSTONE, William Ewart 1809–98. British statesman.
See also with British Prime Ministers page 25.

GLENN, John Herschel b. 1921. American astronaut. The first American to circle the earth in orbit, 1962.

GLINKA, Mikhail Ivanovich 1803–57. Russian composer.
A rare autograph.

GLUCK, Christoph Willibald von 1714–87. Austro-German composer.
Scarce autographically.

GODERICH, Frederick J Robinson, Earl of Ripon, Viscount 1782–1859. British statesman.
See also with British Prime Ministers page 24.

GODOLPHIN, Sidney, Earl of 1645–1712. English statesman. Lord High Treasurer to **Queen Anne**.

GOEBBELS, Joseph 1897–1945. German Nazi politician. **Hitler**'s Propaganda Minister.
Signature as 'Dr. Goebbels'.

GOERING, Hermann W 1893–1946. German Nazi politician and airman. An ace pilot in World War I, he was **Hitler**'s main lieutenant and reorganised the German air force in World War II.

GOETHE, Johann Wolfgang von 1749–1832. German poet, dramatist and scientist. Perhaps the greatest name in German literature.
Goethe's signature varies considerably. Two examples, the first being a rather unusual one. Also MS poem. (British Library.)

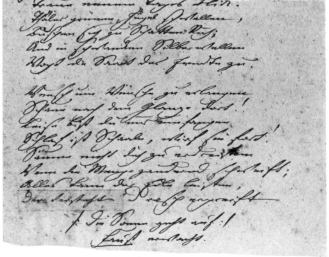

GOGH, Vincent van 1853–90. Dutch post-impressionist painter. His painting signature 'Vincent' and an example of his handwriting. Autographically rare.

Dat is 6 Mei 1870 van hier in commissie gezonden, maar misschien heeft hem het reeds naar Parijs terug gezonden.

Vincent

GOGOL, Nikolai Vasilievich 1809–52. Russian novelist and dramatist.

GOLDSMITH, Oliver 1728–74. Irish-born playwright, poet and novelist. his most famous play was *She Stoops to Conquer*.
A rare and valuable literary autograph.

It is agreed between Goldsmith M. B on one hand and James Dodsley on the other, that Oliver Goldsmith shall write for James Dodsley a book called a Chronological history of the lives of eminent persons of Great Britain.
1763   *Oliver Goldsmith.*

GONCOURT, Edmond de 1822–96. French novelist.

Tout à vous d. coeur
E d. Goncourt

GORDON, Charles George 1833–85. British soldier. 'Chinese Gordon' or 'Gordon of Khartoum'. A man of many parts, he was murdered in Khartoum by the followers of the Mahdi.

GORKI, Maxim (Aleksei Maximovich Peshkov) 1868–1936. Russian writer.

GOUNOD, Charles (F) 1818–93. French composer of *Faust*, etc.
Signed autograph music from the introduction to *Faust*, 1860. (Author's Collection.)

Ch: Gounod
27 Xbre 1860.

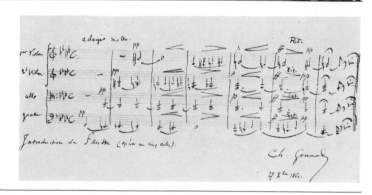

GOUVION SAINT-CYR, Marquis Laurent de 1764–1830. French Marshal and War Minister.
See also with Napoleonic Marshals page 178.

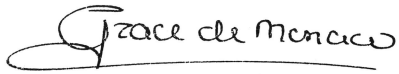

GOYA (Y LUCIENTES), Francisco José de 1746–1828. Spanish master painter.
An example of his painting signature.

GRACE OF MONACO, Princess. Consort of Prince **Rainier**, formerly film actress Grace Kelly.
See also PS with Rainier page 187.

GRACE, W(illiam) G(ilbert) 1848–1915. English cricketer. His name has a permanent place in cricket history.
An ALS concerning a team to play against Australia. 'We are awfully short of bowlers . . . it is very annoying being beaten time after time.' 7 June 1890. (Author's Collection.)

GRAFTON, Augustus H Fitzroy, 3rd Duke of 1735–1811. English statesman.
See also with other British Prime Ministers page 68.

GRAHAME, Kenneth 1859–1922. Scottish writer famed for his children's classic *The Wind in the Willows*.
ALS asking not to be put into *Who's Who*! (Richmond Borough Council Library.)

GRAINGER, Percy Aldridge 1882–1961. Australian-born American composer. Influenced by his friend **Grieg**, he was a keen revivalist of folk music.

GRANT, Ulysses S(impson) 1822–85. American soldier and eighteenth President. See also with US Presidents page 204.

GRAVES, Robert R b. 1895. British poet and novelist. His *I Claudius* won both the Hawthornden and Tait Black prizes.

GRAY, Thomas 1716–71. English poet. Signature; also part of the MSS of his *Elegy in a Country Churchyard* entirely in the holograph of the poet himself. (The British Library.)

'GRECO, El', real name Domenico Theotocopouli 1541–1614. Cretan-born painter who lived and worked at Toledo, Spain.

GREELEY, Horace 1811–72. American writer and politician. Greeley's writing is notoriously unreadable.

GREENAWAY, Kate 1846–1901. English artist famed for her portrayal of children.

GREENE, Graham b. 1904. British novelist and playwright. Works include *The Third Man* and *Brighton Rock*.

GREGORY XIII, Ugo Buoncompagni 1502–85. The Pope, 1572–85, who instituted the reformed Gregorian calendar used to this day. Rare examples of his holograph and signature.

GREGORY XIV, Nicholas Sfondrate 1535–91. Pope, 1590–91, he excommunicated France's great king Henry IV. Autographically rare when signed as Pope, as shown here, because he reigned for less than one year.

GRENFELL, Sir Wilfred T 1865–1940. British medical missionary and explorer in Labrador.

GRENVILLE, George 1712–70. English statesman.
See also with British Prime Ministers page 68.

GRENVILLE, Sir Richard *c.* 1541–91. Heroic British Admiral who with a single small ship, *The Revenge*, fought to the death against a fleet of 53 Spanish sail. Immortalised in **Tennyson**'s poem 'The Revenge'.

GRENVILLE, William Wyndham, Lord 1759–1834. English statesman.
See also with British Prime Ministers page 68.

GRESHAM, Sir Thomas 1519–79. Tudor merchant. Lord Mayor of London. Founder of the Royal Exchange.

GREUZE, Jean Baptiste 1725–1805. French painter.
A rare autograph.

GREY, Charles, 2nd Earl 1764–1845. British statesman whose ministry passed the Reform Bill.
See also with British Prime Ministers page 69.

G

GREY, Lady Jane 1537–54. Queen of England for 11 days, 9 to 19 July 1553, between the death of **Edward VI** and the succession of **Mary I**. Executed. See also with British Sovereigns page 24.

GREY, Zane 1875–1939. American novelist famed for his Western cowboy adventure tales.

GRIEG, Edvard Hagerup 1843–1907. Norway's foremost composer. Signature and an excellent photograph of himself across which he has jokingly written 'This is not Edvard Grieg.' (Author's Collection.)

GRIMALDI, Joseph 1779–1837. The 'classic' English clown who first performed at Drury Lane, at the age of two!

GRIMM, the Brothers Jacob L C 1785–1863 and Wilhelm C 1786–1859. German folk-lorists famed for *Grimms' Fairy Tales*. They were also distinguished philologists.

'GROCK', stage name of Adrien Wettach 1880–1959. The world-famous Swiss clown. A signed self-caricature. (Author's Collection.)

GROPIUS, Walter 1883–1969. German architect. Designed the Bauhaus. Subsequently lived and worked in the USA.

GROTIUS, Hugo. Huig van Groot, 1583–1645. Dutch jurist, theologian and politician. His *De Jure Belli et Pacis* is accepted as being the beginning of the science of international law.

GROUCHY, Emmanuel Marquis de 1766–1847. French Marshal.
See also with Napoleonic Marshals page 178.

GRÜNEWALD, Matthias, or Mathis Nithardt *c.* 1480–1528. German artist, architect and engineer.
An example of the device with which he signed his work.

GUILLOTIN, Joseph Ignace 1738–1814. French Revolutionary physician who proposed, on humanitarian grounds, the decapitating machine named after him.

GUISE, François, Duc de 1519–63. French soldier who took Calais from the English.

GUITRY, Sacha 1885–1957. French actor and dramatist.

GUIZOT, François Pierre G 1787–1874. French statesman. Prime Minister under **Louis Philippe**. A distinguished historian.

GUSTAV(US) II ADOLPHUS, 1594–1632. Sweden's warrior-king. 'The Lion of the North'.

GUSTAV V, 1858–1950. The longest reigning monarch, 1907–50, in Sweden's history.

GUSTAV VI (ADOLF), 1882–1973. King of Sweden 1950–73.
See also 'pig' page 147.

GWINNETT, Button 1735–77. American politician. President of Georgia. Although little known outside the USA, his is the most sought-after of all American autographs. He was a signer of the Declaration of Independence, but the exceptional rarity of his autograph makes a complete collection of these virtually impossible. As long ago as 1927, a holograph letter of Gwinnett sold for $51,000. The value today is incalculable. Variant autographs.

GWYNNE, Nell (Eleanor) 1650–87. The orange girl and minor actress who became **Charles II**'s favourite mistress.
An excessively rare autograph. This handwriting, from the British Museum, cannot be definitely identified as hers. Many authorities think she could only write her initials, as also seen here.

HAAKON VII, 1872–1957. First King of Norway, on its independence from Sweden, 1905–57.

HAECKEL, Ernst Heinrich 1834–1919. German naturalist.

HAGEN, Walter b. 1892. American golfer. Twice winner of the US Open and four times of the British Open Championships.

HAGGARD, Sir (H) Rider 1856–1925. English adventure novelist. Wrote *King Solomon's Mines*, *She*, etc.

HAHN, Otto 1879–1968. German physical chemist. Nobel Prize, 1944 for work on atomic fission.

HAIG, Douglas, 1st Earl 1861–1928. British Field Marshal. C-in-C in France in World War I.

HAILE SELASSIE, 1891–1975. Emperor of Ehtiopia from 1930 until his dethronement in 1974. Known as 'The Lion of Judah', he was formerly Ras Tafari, son of Ras Makonnen.

HAILWOOD, 'Mike' (Stanley Michael Bailey) b. 1940. British racing motor cyclist. At 21 the youngest rider ever to become World Champion (1961).

HAKLUYT, Richard *c*. 1552–1616. English geographer and cosmographer. The Hakluyt Society is named after him.

HALEVY, Jacques 1799–1862. French composer. Perpetual Secretary of the Academy of Fine Arts.

HALLEY, Edmund 1656–1742. English astronomer. Astronomer-Royal 1720. Predicted the return of (Halley's) comet.

HALLOWES, Odette M C b. 1912. 'Odette'. War heroine. Gained the George Cross for her courageous service with the French Resistance in World War II.

HALS, Frans *c.* 1580–1666. Dutch painter. Particularly famed for his *Laughing Cavalier*. Variant signatures from two notarial deeds.

HAMILTON, Emma, Lady *c.* 1765–1815. **Nelson**'s mistress.
A rather scarce autograph.

HANCOCK, John 1737–93. American Revolutionary statesman. 'The First Signer'. President of the Continental Congress 1775–7. First Governor of the State of Massachusetts.

HANDEL, George Frederick 1685–1759. German-born British naturalised composer. His signature in English and German styles.

HARDENBERG, Prince Karl August von 1750–1822. Foreign Minister and Chancellor of Prussia. Amongst his many reforms were the abolition of serfdom and of monopolies and the emancipation of Jews.

HARDIE, J Keir 1856–1915. Scottish politician. A founder of the Labour Party.

HARDING, Warren G 1865–1923. Twenty-ninth President of the USA.
See also with US Presidents page 205.

HARDY, Thomas 1840–1928. English novelist. Author of *Tess of the D'Urbervilles* and *Far from the Madding Crowd*.
ALS concerning one of his poems, 7 April 1906. (Author's Collection.)

From THOS. HARDY,
Max Gate,
Dorchester.

April 7. 1906

Dear Sir: you have my full permission to print "The Going of the Battery" in the series you are planning. Please use a copy the poem as it appears in the Volume entitled "Poems of the Past & Present." as the newspaper form was not quite correct. Yours truly T. Hardy.

Mess.

HARI, Mata. Stage name of Margaretha Zelle 1876–1917. Dutch spy and dancer who was shot for espionage in France in World War I.
A rare autograph.

HARRISON, Benjamin 1833–1901. Twenty-third President of the USA.
See also with US Presidents page 205.

HARRISON, William Henry 1773–1841. Ninth President of the USA. His autograph when President is extremely rare as he only held office for one month, 4 March–4 April 1841. See also with US Presidents page 204.

HARVEY, William 1578–1657. English physician and anatomist. Discovered the circulation of the blood.
Autographically very scarce.

HASTINGS, Warren 1732–1818. British administrator in India and its first Governor-General. His seven-year trial for malpractice ended in his acquittal.

HATTON, Sir Christopher 1540–91. 'The Dancing Chancellor'. A favourite courtier of Queen **Elizabeth**. Lord Chancellor 1587.

H

HAUPTMANN, Gerhart 1862–1946. German novelist and dramatist. Won Nobel Prize, 1912.

HAWKINS (or HAWKYNS), Sir John 1532–95. English sailor. **Drake**'s cousin, he reconstructed the Elizabethan Navy.

HAWTHORNE, Nathaniel 1804–64. American novelist and short-story writer. Wrote *The House of Seven Gables*, *Tanglewood Tales*, etc.
Two widely variant signatures.

HAYDN, (F) Joseph 1732–1809. The famed Austrian composer. Two of his greatest works are *The Creation* and *The Seasons*. Holograph and signed title page of his Canzonettas. (Author's Collection.)

HAYDON, Benjamin Robert 1786–1846. Controversial British historical painter who ended his own life. His outstanding painting is *The Raising of Lazarus*.

HAYES, Rutherford B(irchard) 1822–93. Nineteenth President of the USA. See also signature with US Presidents page 204.

HAZLITT, William 1778–1830. English essayist and literary critic. A powerful controversialist.
Variant autographs.

HEATH, Edward (R G) b. 1916. British Conservative Prime Minister 1970–4. See also with British Prime Ministers page 69.

HEDIN, Sven A 1865–1952. Swedish explorer in Asia. Made the first detailed map of the Gobi desert and Tibet.

HEGEL, Georg Wilhelm F 1770–1831. German idealist philosopher whose work such as *The Science of Logic* and *The Philosophy of Right* still has a profound influence on philosophical thinking.

HEIDEGGER, Martin b. 1889. German philosopher influenced by **Kierkegaard** and himself an influence on **Sartre** with his existentialism.

HEINE, Heinrich 1797–1856. One of Germany's greatest poets.
His autograph in French and German.

HEMINGWAY, Ernest (Millar) 1899–1961. American writer. Works include *A Farewell to Arms*, *For Whom the Bell Tolls* and *The Old Man and the Sea*. Nobel Prize 1954. A much sought-after literary autograph.

HENIE, Sonja 1912–69. Norwegian ice skater and film actress. Three times Olympic and ten times World women's figure skating champion.

HENRY IV, 1367–1413. King of England 1399–1413.
See also with British Sovereigns page 24.

HENRY V, 1387–1422. King of England 1413–22. The victor of Agincourt.
See also with British Sovereigns page 24.

HENRY VI, 1421–71. King of England 1422 until deposed in 1461 by **Edward IV**. Briefly restored by Warwick in 1470, he was soon captured and murdered in the Tower of London.

See also with British Sovereigns page 24.

HENRY VII, 1457–1509. The first of the Tudor sovereigns. King of England 1485–1509.
See also with British Sovereigns page 24.

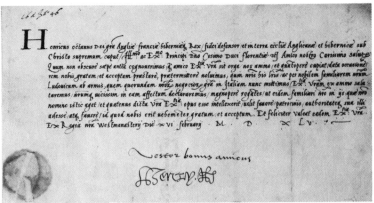

HENRY VIII, 1491–1547. King of England 1509–47. Though cruel and despotic, Henry was a patron of the arts. His 'popular', if such a word can be used in his case, fame today seems to rest in the fact that he had six wives. These are (1) Catherine of Aragon signing as 'Ekatherina, the quene'; (2) Anne Boleyn signed as queen; (3) Jane Seymour, signed as queen; (4) Anne of Cleves, as 'Anna, the dowager of Cleves'; (5) Catherine Howard, her Christian name only; (6) Catherine Parr as 'Katherina Regina, KP (Katherine Parr)', and (7) in totally different handwriting 'Kateryn, the Quene Regente, KP'. The signatures of all the Queens of Henry VIII are rare, those of Jane Seymour, Anne of Cleves and Catherine Howard being excessively so. Above, an LS of Henry himself to the Duke of Florence sending a representative who was in fact intended to murder **Cardinal Pole**, 1545. (Author's Collection.)

HENRY II, 1519–59. King of France 1547–59. Son of **Francis I**, he married **Catherine de Medici(s)**. Three of his sons succeeded to the French throne.

HENRY III, 1551–89. King of France 1574–89.

HENRY IV, 1553–1610. The warrior Henry of Navarre who became King of France in 1589. (1) Normal signature and (2) scarce monogram used when writing to his wife **Marie de Medici**, an interlacing of their initials.

HENRY THE NAVIGATOR, 1394–1460. Prince of Portugal. Responsible for sending navigators and explorers on many voyages. This very rare signature reads 'I.d.a.' (Iffante Dom Anrique) (Henry).

HENRY, Joseph 1797–1878. American physicist. The first secretary of the Smithsonian Institute, he discovered electromagnetic induction, independently of **Faraday**.

'**HENRY, O**' pseudonym of William Sydney Porter 1862–1910. American short-story writer.

HENRY, Patrick 1736–99. American Revolutionary leader. Governor of Virginia. Remembered for his famous words: 'Give me liberty, or give me death.'

HERBERT, Victor 1859–1924. Irish-American composer. Wrote the operetta *Naughty Marietta* and the song 'Ah, sweet mystery of life'.

HERRICK, Robert 1591–1674. English poet. His lyrics include 'Gather ye rosebuds while ye may' and 'Cherry ripe'.

HERSCHEL, Sir John (F W) 1792–1871. English astronomer. Son of **Sir William** (see below). Pioneered celestial photography. He discovered 525 nebulae, and served as Master of the Mint in 1850–55.

HERSCHEL, Sir (F) William 1738–1822. English astronomer. Discovered the planet Uranus.

HERTZOG, James Barry Munnik 1866–1942. South African statesman. Founded the Nationalist Party and was Prime Minister 1924–39.

HESS, Rudolf b. 1894. German Nazi politician. Deputy to **Hitler**. Tried to negotiate an Anglo-German peace at the height of World War II. Imprisoned in Spandau gaol since 1946.

HESSE, Hermann 1877–1962. German author. Won Nobel Prize, 1946. Variant signatures.

HEYERDAHL, Thor b. 1914. Norwegian anthropologist and explorer. Famed for his Pacific voyage on the raft 'Kon-Tiki' and his subsequent book thereon.

HIDEYOSHI, Toyotomi 1536–98. Japanese warrior statesman. Kwampaku (Regent) and military supremo of Japan 1585–91.

HILL, Sir Rowland 1795–1879. The originator, as Secretary to the Post Office, of penny postage.

Sir Rowland's autograph is also sought by collectors of postal history.

Care must be taken to distinguish this from the signatures of Rowland Hill the preacher and Rowland, Lord Hill, the general, who were both his contemporaries.

HILLARY, Sir Edmund b. 1919. New Zealand mountaineer and explorer. With **Tenzing** the first to climb Mount Everest.

HIMMLER, Heinrich 1900–45. German Nazi leader, the head of the dreaded SS. A cold-blooded mass murderer. Over 7 million people were exterminated under his policies.

HINDEMITH, Paul 1895–1963. German composer and violinist.

HINDENBURG (und BENECKENDORFF), Paul von 1847–1934. German Field Marshal and President.

HIROHITO, Emperor b. 1901. Emperor of Japan from 1926. The 124th in direct lineage.

HITCHCOCK, Alfred (J) b. 1899. British-born American film director, known for his 'suspense' films.

HITLER, Adolf 1889–1945. German dictator, known as 'Führer' (Leader). Co-founder of the Nazis, (National Socialists).

HOBBEMA, Meindert 1638–1709. Dutch landscape painter. His masterpiece is *The Avenue, Middelharnis*.
Variant signatures used on his paintings.

HOBBES, Thomas 1588–1679. English philosopher.
A scarce autograph.

HOBBS, Sir John Berry 1882–1963. 'Jack' Hobbs. English cricketer. One of the most successful batsmen of all time. He scored a record 197 centuries in first-class cricket.
See also 'pig' page 147.

HO CHI-MINH, 1892–1969. Vietnamese Communist statesman. Became Prime Minister and, in 1954, President of North Vietnam which he sought to re-unite with South Vietnam by war.

HODLER, Ferdinand 1853–1918. Swiss historical and genre painter.

HOFSTADTER, Robert b. 1915. American physicist. Nobel Prize, 1961 for atomic structure researches.

HOGARTH, William 1697–1764. English painter and engraver. Celebrated for his satirical series such as *A Rake's Progress* and *Marriage à la Mode*.

I have done all I can to the Picture of Sigismunda, you may remember you was pleas'd to say you would give me what price I should think fit.

W. Hogarth

HOLBEIN, Hans 'The Younger' 1497–1543. German painter. One of the great masters of portraiture. In England particularly known for his portraits of **Henry VIII** and his circle.

HÖLDERLIN, (J C) Friedrich 1770–1843. German poet.

HOLMES, Oliver Wendell 1809–94. American writer. His autograph should not be confused with that of his jurist son of the same name.

HOLST, Gustav (T) 1874–1934. English composer of Swedish origin. He wrote two comic operas as well as choral and orchestral works.

HONEGGER, Arthur 1892–1956. Swiss-French composer. One of 'Les Six' group.

HOOD, Samuel, Viscount 1724–1816. British Naval Commander.

HOOVER, Herbert Clark 1874–1964. Thirty-first President of the USA. See also with US Presidents page 205.

'HOPE, Anthony' pseudonym of Sir Anthony Hope Hawkins 1863–1933. English novelist. Wrote *The Prisoner of Zenda*.

HOPE, 'Bob' (Leslie Townes Hope) b. 1904 in Eltham, Kent. American comedian.

HORTHY (de NAGYBANYA), Nicholas 1868–1957. Hungarian admiral and statesman. Regent of Hungary 1920–44.

HOUDIN, (J E) Robert 1805–71. French magician who helped to destroy the influence of the marabouts in Algeria by exposing their supposed 'miracles'. **Houdini** took his pseudonym from him.

'HOUDINI, Harry', real name Erich Weiss 1874–1926. American magician. The most famed of all escapologists. Photograph bearing the words 'Locks, bolts and bars fly asunder when the original of this photo is about!' Signed and dated at Liverpool, 20 October 1904. (Author's Collection.)

HOUDON, Jean Antoine 1741–1828. French sculptor. His portrait sculptures include **Diderot**, **Voltaire**, **Rousseau**, **Molière** and **Napoleon**.

HOUSMAN, Alfred Edward 1859–1936. English poet and scholar known for *A Shropshire Lad*.

Dictionary Names

1.

My Dear Walsingham
For gods sake come to me immediately,
in this moment I have much want
of the comfort of a real friend: poor
Miss Ray was inhumanly murthered
last night as she was stepping into
her coach at the playhouse door

Thursday morning   I am ever yours
7 o'clock.   Sandwich
The Murtherer is taken
& sent to Prison.

2. *De silhouette*

3. *Cardigan*

4. *A E Burnside*

5. *Mesmer*

6. *Yours very truly*
W A Spooner

7. *Votre Camaraden*
Sade

8. *Sacher Masoch*

A small selection of autographs of people whose names have given words to the English dictionary.

1. 4th Earl of Sandwich (sandwich). ALS about the murder of his mistress, Martha Ray. (Public Record Office of Northern Ireland.)
2. Étienne de Silhouette (silhouette).
3. 7th Earl of Cardigan (cardigan).
4. General Burnside (sideburns).
5. F. Mesmer (mesmerism).
6. Dean W A Spooner (spoonerism).
7. Donatien, Marquis de Sade (sadism).
8. L von Sacher Masoch (masochism).

For all biographical details see under individual names in main text.

HOWARD OF EFFINGHAM, Charles, Lord, Earl of Nottingham, 1536–1624. English Naval Commander. As Lord High Admiral commanded against the Spanish Armada, 1588. Signature as 'Not(t)ingham'.

HOWE, Richard Earl 1726–99. British Naval Commander. Victor against the French off Ushant of the battle of 'the Glorious First of June', 1794.

HUGHES, William Morris 1864–1952. Australian statesman. Prime Minister 1915–23.

HUGO, Victor M 1802–85. French man of letters. His many works vary from the classic novel *Les Misérables* to his great stage rhapsodies *Hernani* and *Ruy Blas*.

HUMBOLDT, (F H) Alexander, Baron von 1769–1859. German naturalist and traveller.
Humboldt's somewhat illegible autograph, though not yet scarce, is sought after.

HUMPERDINCK, Engelbert 1854–1921. German composer. Portrait card also showing his house with signed autograph musical quotation from his children's opera *Hansel und Gretel*. Dated Boppard 27 November 1900. (Author's Collection.)

HUNT, John, Lord b. 1910. British mountaineer and soldier. Led the first successful Everest expedition, 1953.

HUNT, (James Henry) Leigh 1784–1859. English poet and essayist. Friend of **Shelley** and **Byron**.

HUNT, William Holman 1827–1910. English Pre-Raphaelite painter of *The Light of the World*, etc.

HUNTER, John 1728–93. Scottish anatomist and surgeon. Considered the founder of scientific surgery.
A scarce autograph.

HUS, or HUSS Johannes (or Jan) *c.* 1369–1415. Bohemian religious reformer. His death by burning as a heretic by the Council of Constance led to the Hussite Wars of 1419–34.

HUSSEIN I, King b. 1935. King of Jordan. Signatures in English and Arabic.

HUXLEY, Aldous (L) 1894–1963. English novelist and essayist. Author of the satirical *Brave New World*, etc. Huxley's signature, though modern, is in demand.
ANS. (Author's Collection.)

HUXLEY, Thomas Henry 1825–95. English biologist and anatomist. Grandfather of **Aldous Huxley** (above).

IBRAHIM PASHA, 1789–1848. Egyptian soldier and statesman. A successful commander of his father, **Mohammed Ali**'s forces against the Wahabis, and his successor as Viceroy.

IBSEN, Henrik 1828–1906. Norwegian dramatist and poet. Author of *Peer Gynt*, *Hedda Gabler*, etc.
Variant autographs.

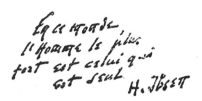

IGNATIUS LOYOLA, Saint (formerly Iñigo de Onez or López de Recalde) 1491–1556. Spanish soldier and ecclesiastic who co-founded the Jesuits.

INDY, Vincent d' 1851–1931. French composer.
Holograph music quotation, signed.
(Author's Collection.)

INGRES, Jean A D 1780–1867. Painter. A leader of the French classicists. An example of his signature from a painting.

INNOCENT XIII, Pope (Michelangelo Conti) 1655–1724. The 245th Pontiff, 1721–4. Granted Naples to the Holy Roman Emperor. Signature as Cardinal.

INÖNÜ, Ismet b. 1884. Turkish statesman and soldier. **Kemal Atatürk**'s right-hand man and his successor as President (1938–50). PS. (Author's Collection.)

IONESCO, Eugene b. 1912. Rumanian-born French dramatist. A master of surrealistic 'dream world' plays.

IRVING, Sir Henry. J H Brodribb 1838–1905. Victorian actor-manager. The first actor to be knighted. The writing above the second signature is identifiable as that of Irving's secretary and partner **Bram Stoker** the author of *Dracula*. It is interesting, autographically, that Stoker often wrote to Irving's dictation.

IRVING, Washington 1783–1859. American writer. The author of *Rip Van Winkle*.

ISABELLA I, 1451–1504. Queen Isabella 'the Catholic', wife, and thus co-ruler of Aragon and Castile, of **Ferdinand V**. With **Ferdinand** the joint patron of **Columbus**. Signature 'Yo La Reyna' – 'I the Queen'.

ISMAIL PASHA, 1830–95. Khedive of Egypt 1863 until deposed in 1879. In 1875 he was forced to dispose of 177,000 shares in the Suez Canal to the British Government of **Disraeli**.

ITO, Prince Hirobumi 1841–1909. Japanese statesman (four times Prime Minister) who drafted the Japanese constitution. Not to be confused with **Count Ito**, the Admiral.

ITO, Count Yuko 1843–1914. Japanese Admiral. C-in-C in Chinese-Japanese War and Chief of Naval Staff throughout the Russo-Japanese War.
Signature in Japanese as Viscount and Admiral. He should not be confused with Prince **Ito**, preceding.

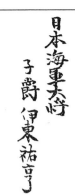

IVAN IV, The Terrible 1530–84. The first Russian ruler to use the title of 'tsar'. An autocrat and tyrant who killed his own son in a fit of rage and died of sorrow at the deed three years later.

JACKSON, Andrew 1767–1845. Seventh President of the USA.
See also signature with US Presidents page 204.

JACKSON, Thomas Jonathan 'Stonewall' 1824–63. American Confederate general so nicknamed for his dogged stand at Bull Run in the American Civil War.

JAMES I (VI of Scotland), 1566–1625. King of Scotland from 1567 on the abdication of his mother **Mary Queen of Scots**, and of Great Britain 1603–25.
See also with British Sovereigns page 24.

JAMES II, 1633–1701. British king. Succeeded 1685 but, alienated from his subjects by unacceptable religious policies, was forced to vacate the throne, 1688. James II's signature as King is becoming scarce.

JAMES II, 1430–60. King of Scotland 1437–60.
Autographically interesting as being the earliest Scottish Sovereign whose signature is known to have survived.

JAMES V, King 1512–42. King of Scotland 1513–42. Father of **Mary Queen of Scots** and grandfather of **James I** of England (VI of Scotland).

J

JAMES, Henry 1843–1916. American-born, British naturalised novelist. Not to be confused with either Henry James, the politician, or Sir Henry James, the military engineer.

JANE GREY, Queen – see **GREY**. Executed in the Tower of London aged 16. Also see with British Sovereigns page 24.

JANE SEYMOUR, Queen *c*. 1509–37. Third Queen of Henry VIII and mother of **Edward VI**. Also see under Henry VIII.

JASPERS, Karl 1883–1969. German existentialist philosopher and psychologist.

JEFFERSON, Thomas 1743–1826. Third President of the USA. Amongst other features of his administration was the Purchase of Louisiana in 1803. Earlier he had been responsible for drawing up the Declaration of Independence. Also see with US Presidents page 204.

JEFFREYS, George, Lord 1648–89. The infamous judge at the 'Bloody Assize' after **Monmouth**'s rebellion, 1685. He signs 'C' (Cancellarius) after his name as Lord Chancellor.

JELLICOE, John Rushworth, Earl 1859–1935. British Admiral-of-the-Fleet, prominent in World War I. Governor of New Zealand 1920–4.

JENNER, Edward 1749–1823. The discoverer of vaccination.
Two examples of this important and rather scarce autograph are shown here.

JEROME, Jerome K 1859–1927. English novelist and playwright. Known for his humorous masterpiece *Three Men in a Boat*. See also 'pig' page 147.

JIMÉNEZ, Juan Ramon 1881–1958. Spanish lyric poet.

JINNAH, Quaid-i-Azim Mahomed Ali. 1876–1948. The Founder of the State of Pakistan and its first Governor-General.

JOACHIM, Joseph 1831–1907. Hungarian violinist and composer. Holograph music extract with signed autograph dedication. (Author's Collection.)

JOAN I (JOANNA), Juana 'la Loca' – 'the Mad' 1475–1555. Queen of Castile and Leon. Daughter of **Ferdinand V** and **Isabella** and mother of the Emperor **Charles V**. After two years of rule, she fell into deep melancholy developing into madness on the death of her husband, and her father Ferdinand V had to act as regent for her. Variant signatures 'Yo la Reyna' ('I the Queen'), one evidently during madness.

J

JOAN OF ARC, Saint 1412–31. Jeanne d'Arc, 'the Maid of Orleans', 'La Pucelle'. French national heroine, warrior, martyr and saint. The signatures from her two known letters (to the people of Reims), of 16 March and 28 March 1430, respectively. In both the signature is in a different hand from the body of the letter and could be entirely autograph, but most authorities consider that only the 'J' in each case is in her own hand. The earlier letter is shown in full.

JOHN OF THE CROSS (originally Juan de Yepis y Alvarez), Saint 1542–91. Spanish Saint and mystic. Founder with **Saint Teresa** of the Discalced Carmelites.

JOHN XXIII, Pope Angelo Giuseppe Roncalli 1881–1963. The 262nd Pontiff of the Church of Rome 1958–63. Promoted reconciliation with other Churches. Signature from a letter whilst Papal Nuncio to France.

JOHN, Augustus 1878–1961. British painter.

JOHN OF AUSTRIA, Don 1547–78. Spanish General and Admiral. The natural son of the Emperor **Charles V**, he won the great sea battle of Lepanto against the Turks 1571.
(1) Usual signature; (2) uncommon signature with full title.

JOHNSON, Amy 1903–41. British aviatrix. Made several solo flight records, England to Australia, to Cape Town, etc. Drowned on active service.

JOHNSON, Andrew 1808–75. Seventeenth President of the USA.
See also with US Presidents page 204.

JOHNSON, Jack 1878–1946. American negro boxer. World Champion 1908–15.

JOHNSON, Lyndon Baines 1908–72. Thirty-sixth President of the USA.
See also with US Presidents page 205.

JOHNSON, Samuel 1709–84. Doctor Johnson. English lexicographer, conversationalist and critic.
A literary autograph of major importance. ANS. (The British Library.)

JONES, Inigo 1573–1652. British architect of Whitehall Banqueting Hall and other London buildings. He designed Covent Garden and Lincoln's Inn Fields.

JONES, John Paul 1747–92. Scottish-born American sailor. Famed for his daring exploits in the American War of Independence and later as an Admiral in the Russian fleet against Turkey.

JONES, Robert T ('Bobby') 1902–71. American golfer. Won the US Open and Amateur and the British Open and Amateur Championships all in the same year, 1930.

J

JONSON, Ben 1572–1637. English dramatist and poet. Author of *Volpone* and *The Alchemist*; also of lyric songs, including 'Drink to me only with thine eyes'.

Examples of his autograph showing (1) his sloping hand, and (2) his more upright and careful writing.

JOSÉPHINE, Empress (*née* Marie Joséphine Tascher de la Pagerie, later Beauharnais) 1763–1814. First wife and consort of Napoleon. Signature only is hers.

JOURDAN, Jean-Baptiste, Comte 1762–1833. French soldier.
See also with Napoleonic Marshals page 178.

JOYCE, James (Augustine Aloysius) 1882–1941. Irish author of *Ulysses* and *Portrait of the Artist as a Young Man*.
Autographically uncommon.

JOYCE, William 1906–46. The British traitor, 'Lord Haw-haw', who broadcast from Germany in World War II.

JUAN CARLOS I, b. 1938. King of Spain after the death of General **Franco**, 1975. Grandson of **Alfonso XIII**.

JUANTORENA, Alberto b. 1951. Cuban athlete. Double gold medallist in 1976 Olympics.

JUAREZ, Benito (Pablo) 1806–72, Mexican patriot and statesman. Several times President.

JULIANA, Queen b. 1909. Queen of the Netherlands, 1948. She succeeded on the abdication of her mother Queen Wilhelmina.

JULIUS II, Pope Giuliano della Rovere 1443–1513. The 217th Pontiff (1503–13). A natural warrior, he made war against Venice and France yet was a patron of the arts.

JUNG, Carl Gustav 1875–1961. Swiss psychiatrist. An early associate of **Freud**, he was the founder of analytical psychology in which he developed the theory of complexes. A signed autograph note in a book. (By courtesy of Miss Ruth Bailey.)

KAFKA, Franz 1883–1924. Austrian Jewish psychological and philosophical writer. A youthful signature and his mature autograph.

KANDINSKY, Vasily 1866–1944. Russian painter. One of the foremost pioneers of the abstract in art.

KANO, Jigoro. Devised ju-jitsu, from which judo developed, by reviving the old fighting arts of Japan, 1882. He came to Britain in 1905 to instruct the first ju-jitsu club in the country at Cambridge University.

KANT, Immanuel 1724–1804. German transcendental philosopher and metaphysician.
An important and sought-after autograph.

KARLOFF, Boris (William H Pratt) 1887–1969. British actor known for his 'horror' roles such as that of Frankenstein's monster.

KASTLER, Alfred b. 1902. French physicist. Nobel Prize, 1966 for work on the development of lasers.

KAUNDA, Kenneth D b. 1924. Zambian statesman. First President, 1964, after having been his country's first Prime Minister.

KAUNITZ, Prince Wenzel Anton von 1711–94. Austrian statesman. Chancellor of Austria for nearly 40 years.

KAZANTZAKIS, Nikos 1884–1957. Greek writer of *Zorba the Greek*, etc.

KEAN, Edmund *c.* 1789–1833. English actor, the most outstanding of his day.

KEATS, John 1795–1821. English poet. Keats' early death has made his autograph a rarity. Also part of the manuscript *Hyperion*. (The British Library.)

KEINO, Kipchoge b. 1940. Kenyan Olympic champion at 1500 metres in 1968 and 3000 metres Steeplechase in 1972.

KEITEL, Wilhelm 1882–1946. German Nazi Field-Marshal and Commander-in-Chief.

KELLER, Helen A 1880–1968. Deaf and blind lecturer, writer and scholar. Taught to speak by Anne Macy.

KELLERMANN, François E C, Duke of Valmy 1735–1820. Marshal of the French Empire.
See also with Napoleon's Marshals page 178.

KELVIN, William Thomson, Lord 1824–1907. Scottish physicist, mathematician and scientific inventor. Famed for his work on hydrodynamics, his electrometers and his researches into thermodynamics.

KEMBLE, Charles 1775–1854. British actor. Excelled in comedy and Shakespearean roles.

KEMPIS, Thomas à c. 1379–1471. German theologian, monk and mystic. Famed as the writer of the treatise *On the Imitation of Christ*. A portion of the holograph manuscript of *On the Imitation of Christ* in the Royal Library, Brussels.

KENNEDY, John F(itzgerald) 1917–63. Thirty-fifth President of the USA. Assassinated at Dallas, Texas.
See signature with US Presidents at page 205. Genuine Kennedy autographs are scarce since he allowed considerable use of the autopen and the copying of his signature by secretaries. This example is from the Library of Congress, Washington, D.C.

KENYATTA, Jomo b. *c*. 1889. Kenyan national leader. First President of Kenya, 1964.

KEPLER, Johann(es) 1571–1630. German astronomer who evolved the three (Kepler's) laws of planetary motion.

KERENSKY, Alexandr F 1881–1970. Russian Revolutionary statesman. Prime Minister after the fall of the Tsar, July–November 1917. Too moderate, he was overthrown by the Bolsheviks.

KETÈLBEY, Albert W 1875–1959. British composer, famed for such works as *In a Monastery Garden* and *In a Persian Market*. Holograph signed extract from both. (Author's Collection.)

KEYNES, John Maynard, Lord 1883–1946. English economist. His autograph – rather exceptionally amongst economists – is in demand.

KHAMA, Sir Seretse b. 1921. Botswana national leader and its first President, 1966.

KHRUSHCHEV, Nikita S 1894–1971. Soviet statesman. First Secretary of the Communist Party, 1953–64 and Premier of the USSR, 1958–64.

KIERKEGAARD, Søren Aabye 1813–55. Danish philosopher and theologian whose theories influenced modern existentialism.

KIESINGER, Kurt Georg b. 1904. West German statesman (Christian Democrat). Chancellor 1966–9.

KILLY, Jean-Claude b. 1943. French skiing champion. Winner of three gold medals in the 1968 Olympics.

KING, Martin Luther 1929–68. American Negro clergyman and civil rights leader. Won Nobel Peace Prize, 1964. Assassinated in Memphis.

KING, William L Mackenzie 1874–1950. Canadian Liberal statesman. Prime Minister, in three terms of office, for a total of 22 years.

KINGSLEY, Charles 1819–75. British novelist, clergyman and historian. Known for his novel *Westward Ho!* and his children's classic *The Water Babies*.

KIPLING, Rudyard 1865–1936. English novelist and poet. His popular works include *The Jungle Book*, *Kim* and the *Just So Stories* for children as well as the poems 'Mandalay' and 'Gunga Din'. Won Nobel Prize, 1907. Variant autographs. Also a PS. (Peter Lawrence's Pictorial Nostalgic Library.)

KISSINGER, Henry Alfred b. 1923. American statesman. As Secretary of State, a tireless worker for peace, for which he was awarded the Nobel Prize in 1973.
A youthful example of his signature.

KITCHENER OF KHARTOUM, Horatio Herbert, 1st Earl 1850–1916. British soldier. Sirdar of Egypt. C-in-C in the South African War. Lost at sea when Minister for War in World War I.

KLEE, Paul 1879–1940. Individualist Swiss painter of the fantastic and abstract. From 1920 to 1932 he taught at the Bauhaus.

KLEIST, (B) Heinrich (W) von 1777–1811. German dramatist and poet.

KNELLER, Sir Godfrey 1646–1723. Dutch-born English portrait painter. Court painter to the British Sovereigns from **Charles II** to **George I**.

KNOX, John 1505–72. Scottish religious reformer. Established Presbyterianism after returning to Scotland from Switzerland where he had associated with Calvin.

KOCH, Robert 1843–1910. German bacteriologist. Discovered the cholera germ and isolated the anthrax and tuberculosis bacilli. Won Nobel Prize, 1905.

KODÁLY, Zoltan 1882–1967. Hungarian composer. Collaborated with **Bartók** on a collection of Hungarian folk-songs.

KOESTLER, Arthur b. 1905. Hungarian-born writer. As a reporter in the Spanish Civil War, imprisoned under death sentence by **Franco**. Wrote the powerful political novel *Darkness at Noon*.

KOKOSCHKA, Oskar b. 1886. Austrian-born British expressionist painter, dramatist and poet.

K

KOSCIUSZKO, Tadeusz A B 1746–1817. Polish soldier and patriot. Fought for the American colonists against Britain and for his country against Russia.

KOSSUTH, Lajos 1802–94. Hungarian patriot. Spent a lifetime of struggle for Hungarian independence from Austria.

KOSYGIN, Alexei Nikolayvich b. 1904. Soviet statesman. Succeeded **Khrushchev** as Premier in 1964.
An uncommon modern autograph.

KREISLER, Fritz 1875–1962. Austrian-born American naturalised violinist and composer.

KŘENEK, Ernst b. 1900. American composer, born in Austria of Czech-German descent. The son-in-law of **Mahler**. His most successful work is perhaps the jazz opera *Johnny strikes up*.
Signed autograph music extract. (Author's Collection. By permission of Mr Křenek.)

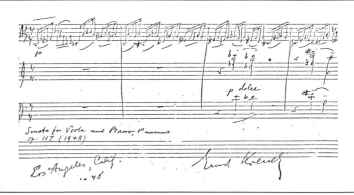

KRIGE, Uys b. 1910. South African poet and playwright.
See PS with other South African writers page 35.

KROPOTKIN, Prince Petr A 1842–1921. Russian revolutionary, geographer and social philosopher.

KRUGER, (Stephanus Johannes) Paul(us) 1825–1904. 'Oom Paul', South African statesman. Founded and was President of the Transvaal state (South African Republic).
Kruger's autograph is uncommon, and is mostly found in signature form only on state documents.

KRUPP (von BOHLEN und HALBACH), Alfred A F 1907–67. German steel manufacturer. Grandson of the founder of the great Krupp steel industrial empire.

KUBELIK, Jan 1880–1940. Czech-born Hungarian violinist and composer.

LACOSTE, René b. 1904. French Lawn Tennis Champion. Winner of the Men's Singles Championship at Wimbledon in 1925 and 1928.

LAFAYETTE, Marie Joseph P Y R G Motier, Marquis de 1757–1834. French soldier, politician and reformer. An associate of **Washington**, he fought for the American cause in the War of Independence and later struggled for constitutional reform in his homeland.

LA FONTAINE, Jean de 1621–95. French poet and writer. Famed for his *Fables*.
An important French literary autograph.

LAGERKVIST, Pär b. 1891. Swedish man of letters. Won Nobel Prize, 1951 for his novel *Barabbas*. ANS 1946. (Royal Swedish Library, Stockholm.)

L

LAGERLÖF, Selma 1858–1940. Swedish novelist. Won Nobel Prize, 1909 for her fairy stories and romances.

LAMARTINE, Alphonse M L de 1790–1869. French poet, historian, orator and politician.

LAMB, Charles 1775–1834. English essayist and critic.

His usual autograph, an ANS to **Robert Southey** (British Library) and an autograph as 'Elia', the name with which he signed his famous *Essays of Elia*.

LANDOR, Walter Savage 1775–1864. English writer of plays, critiques and poems.

LANDSEER, Sir Edwin (Henry) 1802–73. British animal painter.

A typical example of his extrovert autograph.

LANG, Andrew 1844–1912. Scottish man of letters.

LANG, Anton. German carpenter and actor in Oberammergau known for his role as Christ in the Passion Play.

LANGTREY, 'Lillie' 1853–1929. Lady de Bathe. English actress and beauty. 'The Jersey Lily'.

LANNES, Jean, Duke de Montebello 1769–1809. French Marshal. A dashing cavalry leader.
See also with Napoleonic Marshals page 178.

LAS CASAS, Bartolomé de 1474–1566. 'The Apostle of the Indies'. Spanish missionary and historian. Wrote *Historia de las Indias* and the record of the discovery of America by **Columbus** with whom he had sailed on his third voyage.
Signature as Bishop 'Ob(is)po' of Chiapa.

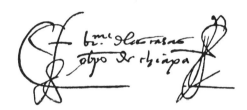

LATIMER, Hugh *c.* 1485–1555. English Protestant martyr. Burned at the stake during the rule of the Catholic 'Bloody' **Mary I**.
Autograph as 'Latymer' and as Bishop of Worcester (Wygorn).

LAUD, William 1573–1645. Archbishop of Canterbury. Beheaded on a doubtful charge of treason.
Signed as Archbishop 'W. Cant(uar)'.

L

LAUDER, Sir Harry 1870–1950. Scottish comedian, singer and song composer of 'Roamin' in the Gloamin'', etc.
Self-caricature. (Author's Collection.)

LAUREL, Stanley and HARDY, Oliver. The popular duo of American film comedians. PS. (Author's Collection.)

LAURIER, Sir Wilfrid 1841–1919. Canadian statesman. The first French-Canadian to become Prime Minister (1896) of his country.

LAVATER, Johan Kaspar 1741–1801. Swiss mystic, poet, philosopher and theologian.
Brief examples of his autograph in French and German.

LAVER, Rod(ney) (George) b. 1938. Australian Lawn Tennis player. Four times Wimbledon Singles Champion.

LAVOISIER, Antoine Laurent 1743–94. French chemist. The founder of modern chemistry. Made experiments leading to the identification and naming of oxygen. A rare and important scientific autograph.

LAW, Andrew Bonar 1858–1923. British statesman.
See also with British Prime Ministers page 69.

LAWRENCE, D(avid) H(erbert) 1885–1930. Controversial British author of *Sons and Lovers*, *Lady Chatterley's Lover*, etc. D H Lawrence's autograph is much in demand.

LAWRENCE, Sir Thomas 1769–1830. English painter. The son of an inn-keeper he became the premier portraitist of his day and President of the Royal Academy.

LAWRENCE, T(homas) E(dward) 1888–1935. 'Lawrence of Arabia'. British soldier, scholar and author of *The Seven Pillars of Wisdom*.
Autographs of Lawrence of Arabia are uncommon and much sought after. Examples shown are an ANS re: circulation of the *Seven Pillars* (Author's Collection) and a signature, whilst seeking anonymity, as 'T E Shaw'. His signature can also be found as 'Ross'.

LAXNESS, Halldór K b. 1902. Icelandic novelist. Won Nobel Prize, 1955. His works include *Salka Valka* and *The Fish Can Sing*.

L

LEACOCK, Stephen (Butler) 1869–1944. Canadian humorist and economist. Head of the economics department of McGill University.

LEAR, Edward 1812–88. English humorous writer and artist. Famed for his self-illustrated *A Book of Nonsense*.

LEE, Robert E 1807–70. American soldier. Commander-in-Chief of the Confederate Army in the American Civil War.
His signature as Captain.

LEFEBVRE, François Joseph, Duke of Danzig 1755–1820. French Marshal.
See also with Napoleonic Marshals page 178.

LEHÁR, Franz 1870–1948. Hungarian composer of operettas, *The Merry Widow*, etc. Autograph musical bars from *Giuditta* and PS. (Author's Collection.)

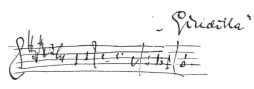

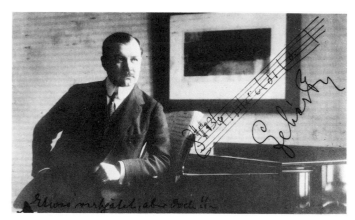

LEIBNIZ, Gottfried Wilhelm, Baron von 1646–1716. German intellectual, philosopher, mathematician, theologian, historian and essayist.

LEICESTER, Robert Dudley, Earl of *c.* 1532–88. English courtier. For many years the favourite of Queen **Elizabeth I**.

LEIGHTON, Frederic, Lord 1830–96. British painter.

Leighton's flamboyant signature was often much larger than this example. He was the first painter to be made a peer but his signature in that rank does not exist as he died the day after his ennoblement.

LELY, Sir Peter (originally Pieter van der Faes) 1618–80. Dutch artist who became Court portrait painter to **Charles I**, **Cromwell** and **Charles II**.

LENGLEN, Suzanne 1899–1938. French Lawn Tennis player. Won all major Ladies championships of her day, including six Wimbledon Singles titles. Regarded by many as the greatest woman player of all time.

LENIN (formerly ULYANOV), Vladimir Ilyich 1870–1924. Russian Revolutionary statesman. Founder of Soviet Union. Assumed name Lenin in 1896. A rare signature of the greatest autographic importance.

LENO, Dan (real name George Galvin) 1860–1904. English comedian.

LEO X, Giovanni de Medici, Pope 1475–1521. The 218th Pontiff (1513–21). Excommunicated **Luther** and was the patron of **Raphael**. He was responsible for planning the rebuilding of St Peters, Rome.

L

LEO XIII, Gioacchino Vincenzo Pecci, Pope 1810–1903. The 257th Pontiff (1878–1903).

LEONCAVALLO, Ruggiero 1858–1919. Italian composer of the opera *I Pagliacci*.

LEONOV, Alexei Arkhipovich b. 1934. Russian cosmonaut. A colonel in the USSR air force, he was the first man to walk in space, 18 March 1965, and in July 1975 commanded the Soviet crew in the Apollo-Soyuz American-Russian docking mission, the first ever link-up in space. Signature and PS. with those of both link-up crews. (NASA photo, Author's Collection.)

LEOPARDI, Giacomo 1798–1837. Italian lyric poet. A lifetime invalid, Leopardi's early death contributes to the scarcity of his autograph.

LEOPOLD II, 1835–1909. King of the Belgians 1865–1909. His backing of Sir **H M Stanley** in his African explorations, led to the founding of the (Belgian) Congo State.

LERMONTOV, Mikhail Yurevich 1814–41. Russian lyric poet and novelist. His greatest works include the verse play *Masquerade* and the novel *A Hero of our Time*. A rare autograph.

LESSEPS, Ferdinand M, Vicomte de 1805–94. French engineer. Built the Suez Canal and planned the Panama Canal.

LESSING, Gotthold Ephraim 1729–81. German critic and dramatist. Known for his critical treatise *Laokoon* and his great tragedy *Emilia Galotti*.

LEWIS, (H) Sinclair 1885–1951. American novelist, playwright and satirist. The first American to win the Nobel Literature Prize, 1930.

LIBERACE, b. 1919. American pianist. Has been the world's highest paid musician, earning $138,000 (£68,000) for one night's performance.
An extrovert example of his signature incorporating his piano.

LIEBIG, Justus, Freiherr von 1803–73. German chemist. Founder of agricultural chemistry and a discoverer of chloroform. Signature as 'Fr(eiherr) Liebig'. He also signed 'Dr. Justus Liebig'.

LI HUNG-CHANG 1823–1901. Chinese statesman. 'The Bismarck of Asia'. Prime Minister, Viceroy of Chihli.
His uncommon signature in Chinese and English.

L

LINCOLN, Abraham 1809–65. Sixteenth President of the USA. Steered his country through its civil war. Assassinated by actor John Wilkes Booth. Highly desirable autograph. See also with US Presidents page 204.

LIND (-GOLDSCHMIDT), Jenny 1820–87. One of the greatest sopranos of all time. Known as 'the Swedish Nightingale', she was, in fact, naturalised British. Married Otto Goldschmidt – see signature.

LINDBERGH, Charles Augustus 1902–74. American aviator. First to fly solo non-stop across the Atlantic, 1927. Lindbergh's autograph is a modern rarity as he had strong fears of it getting into the wrong hands.

LINNAEUS, Carolus. Carl von Linné 1707–78. Swedish botanist. Founder of modern botany, he established the nomenclature system of classification. Variant autographs. (Linnean Society of London.)

LIPPI (or LIPPO), Fra Filippo *c.* 1406–69. Italian religious painter.
Signature as 'Frater Filippo, Florentine painter'.

LISTER, Joseph, Lord 1827–1912. English surgeon who founded antiseptic surgery.

LISZT, Franz 1811–86. Hungarian composer and pianist. Friend, patron and father-in-law of **Wagner**.

LIVERPOOL, Robert Banks Jenkinson, 2nd Earl of 1770–1828. Prime Minister during and after the Napoleonic Wars.
See also with British Prime Ministers page 68.

LIVINGSTONE, David 1813–73. Scottish missionary and explorer in Africa. Discovered Lakes Nyasa and Ngami and the Victoria Falls.

His usual signature together with a rare early one before he added the 'e' to his surname. It is interesting to note that his writing became very much larger as he grew older. Both examples shown are full size.

LLOYD-GEORGE, David, Earl 1863–1945. Welsh Liberal statesman. Prime Minister of Britain 1916–22.

See also with British Prime Ministers page 69.

LOCKE, John 1632–1704. English philosopher and empiricist. With Sir **Francis Bacon**, the founder of empiricism.

LONDON, Jack 1876–1916. American writer of adventure novels, including *the Call of the Wild*, *White Fang* and *The Sea Wolf*.

LONGFELLOW, Henry Wadsworth 1807–82. American poet.

Signed holograph verse from his poem 'The Day is Done'. (Author's Collection.)

LOREN, Sophia b. 1934. Italian film actress (*née* Sofia Scicolone).

LOTI, Pierre. Pseudonym of L M J Viaud. 1850–1923. French novelist.

L

LOUIS XI, 1423–83. King of France 1461–83. A man of cunning and a psychological fear of death, he curtailed the power of the nobles. A patron of the arts and sciences, he founded several universities.

LOUIS XII, 1462–1515. King of France 1498–1515. A just ruler. Known as 'Le Père du Peuple'.

LOUIS XIII, 1601–43. King of France 1610–43. His autocratic mother, **Marie de Medici**, ruled as regent until 1617. Much influenced by his chief Minister, **Richelieu**.

LOUIS XIV, 1638–1715. King of France 1643–1715. 'Le Roi Soleil' (the Sun King). France's most famous monarch.
It was the practice of the Bourbon Kings to approve petitions, etc., with the holograph word 'bon' as seen here (See also **Louis XVI** below). **Napoleon** however used the word 'approuvé' often abbreviated to 'ap'.

LOUIS XV, 1710–74. King of France 1715–74. The expenses of mismanaged wars and the lavish gifts to his mistresses Mesdames **de Pompadour** and **Du Barry** brought the French economy to its knees.

LOUIS XVI, 1754–93. King of France 1774–92. This luckless monarch who married **Marie Antoinette** was caught up in the aftermath of the misrule of his predecessor **Louis XV**. The French Revolution brought about his dethronement and subsequent execution.
Louis XVI's authentic signature (see remarks re: signatures of Kings of France in the Preface page viii) is easily identified since it is so unusual that no secretary attempted to copy it.

LOUIS XVII, 1785–95. The French King who never ruled. His very rare signature reads 'Louis Charles Capet' using the family surname.

LOUIS XVIII, 1755–1824. King of France on the restoration of the Bourbons after the fall of **Napoleon**, 1814–24.

à venir auprès de moi, de vous appeller d'Angleterre)

Louis.

LOUIS, Joe (formerly Joseph Louis Barrow) b. 1914. American boxer. 'The Brown Bomber'. Undefeated World Heavyweight Champion 1937–49.

LOUIS PHILIPPE, 1773–1850. King of France 1830–48. Son of 'Louis Égalité', Duke of Orleans. Became King after the revolution against Charles X but was himself dethroned by the revolution of 1848.

Louis Philippe

LOUVOIS, François M. le Tellier Marquis de 1641–91. **Louis XIV**'s War Minister.

LOWELL, James Russell 1819–91. American poet, essayist and diplomat.
End of an ALS to the author's grandfather, written when Lowell was US Minister in London, 1881. (Author's Collection.)

LUDENDORFF, Erich von 1865–1937. German General. A brilliant strategist, he was Chief of Staff to **Hindenburg** in World War I.

LUDWIG I, 1786–1868. King of Bavaria 1825–48. An eccentric and extravagant ruler, he fell under the influence of favourites, notably **Lola Montez** and was forced to abdicate. Signature in Italian 'Lodovici'.

L - M

LULLY, Jean Baptiste 1632–87. Italian-born French composer.
A rare autograph.

LUTHER, Martin 1483–1546. German religious reformer. The initiator of the Reformation in Germany and thus virtually the first Protestant.

LUTHULI, Albert (John) 1899–1967. African political leader in South Africa. Dedicated to the cause of non-violent resistance, he deplored violent racialism and was awarded the Nobel Peace Prize, 1961. PS *Natal Mercury*. (Author's Collection.)

LYAUTEY, Louis (H G) 1854–1934. French Marshal and colonial administrator. ANS, Paris 13 November 1931. (Author's Collection.)

LYONS, Joseph (Aloysius) 1879–1939. Australian Labour statesman. Prime Minister 1932–9.

MacARTHUR, Douglas 1880–1964. American soldier. Supreme Commander in the S.W. Pacific during World War I. General of the Army, 1944.

MACAULAY, Thomas Babington, Lord 1800–59. British poet, historian and politician. Wrote *The Lays of Ancient Rome*.

MACDONALD, Jacques E J Alexandre, Duke of Taranto 1765–1840. French Marshal of Scottish descent.
See also with Napoleonic Marshals page 178.

MACDONALD, James Ramsay 1866–1937. The first British Labour Prime Minister.
See also with British Prime Ministers page 69.

MacDONALD, Sir John (Alexander) 1815–91. The first Prime Minister of the Dominion of Canada.

McBRIDE, Willie John b. 1940. Irish Rugby (Union) footballer. Holds the World Record of 80 for international appearances. He has played for Ireland 63 times.

MACHADO DE ASSIZ, Joaquim Maria 1839–1908. Brazilian author.

MACHIAVELLI, Niccolo di Bernado dei 1469–1527. Florentine statesman, historiographer and political philosopher. The adjective 'machiavellian' derives from his name. A scarce and important autograph.

McKINLEY, William 1843–1901. Twenty-fifth President of the USA. Shot by an anarchist.
See also with US Presidents page 205.

MACMAHON, Comte Marie Edmé P M de 1808–93. French Marshal. President of the Third Republic 1873–9.

MACMILLAN, (M) Harold b. 1894.
British Conservative Prime Minister.
See also with British Prime Ministers page
69.

MacNEICE, Louis 1907–63. British poet.
Born in Northern Ireland. Known also for
his verse plays and literary criticisms.

MACREADY, W(illiam) C(harles)
1793–1873. British actor. Also manager,
successively, of Covent Garden and Drury
Lane Theatre.

MADISON, James 1751–1836. Fourth
President of the USA.
Also see with US Presidents page 204.

MAETERLINCK, Count Maurice
1862–1949. Belgian dramatist and poet.
Won Nobel Prize, 1911. Wrote the play
Pelléas et Mélisande on which **Debussy** based
his opera.

MAGELLAN, Ferdinand (Fernão de
Magalhães) *c.* 1480–1521. Portuguese navigator. Rounded South America through the
straits now named after him but was killed in
the Philippines, which he had discovered;
thus being prevented from becoming the first
circumnavigator. The voyage was completed by his lieutenant, **Sebastian del
Cano**.

MAHLER, Gustav 1860–1911. Czech-
Austrian composer.
The final holograph lines of a ballad, 1879
and a somewhat different signature.

MAILER, Norman b. 1923. American novelist. Wrote *The Naked and the Dead*.

MAINTENON, Françoise d'Aubigné, Marquise de 1635–1719. Mistress and second wife of **Louis XIV**.

MAKARIOS III, Michael C Mouskos 1913–77. Greek-Cypriot Archbishop and statesman. President of Cyprus, 1959–77.

MALENKOV, Georgi b. 1902. Successor to **Stalin** as Premier of the USSR, 1953 until his downfall, 1955.

MALHERBE, François de 1555–1628. French poet.

MALTHUS, Thomas Robert 1766–1834. English political economist. Though Malthusianism is named after him it is not based on his theories.
A rare autograph.

MANET, Édouard 1832–83. Leading French impressionist painter. One of his later masterpieces is *Bar at the Folies Bergères*.

MANN, Thomas 1875–1955. German man of letters. Won Nobel Prize, 1929.
His signature in English and German styles.

MANNERHEIM, Baron C Gustav E 1867–1951. Finnish patriot, soldier and statesman. President 1944–6.

MANSFIELD, Katherine, pseudonym of K M Murry 1888–1923. New Zealand-born, British short-story writer.
Her autograph is scarce partly owing to her short life. Part ALS with nickname Tiger.

MANZONI, Alessandro (F T A) 1785–1873. Italian novelist and poet. His *I Promessi Sposi* has been described as the most notable novel in Italian literature. As a result his autograph, though not strictly scarce, is sought after.

MAO TSE-TUNG 1893–1976. Former leader of the Chinese people. Chairman of the Chinese Communist Party. One of the several variations of his very rare signature.

MARAT, Jean Paul 1743–93. A doctor, he was one of the most bloodthirsty of the French Revolutionary leaders. Murdered in his bath by **Charlotte Corday**. Two examples of this scarce French autograph.

MARCIANO, 'Rocky' 1923–69. American undefeated World Heavyweight Boxing Champion, 1952–6.

MARCONI, Guglielmo, Marchese 1874–1937. Italian physicist and electrical engineer. First successful pioneer of wireless. Won Nobel Prize for Physics, 1909.

In the latter part of the last and the earlier years of this century, many people kept pig books, much as they did autograph albums, filled with drawings of pigs done blindfold. Here are some amusing examples drawn and signed by famous men from a pig book, 1896–1935. (Author's Collection.)

The 'artists' are:

1. King Carlos I of Portugal.
2. Sir Jack Hobbs.
3. Herbert, Lord Austin.
4. King Gustav (Adolf) VI of Sweden.
5. Robert, Lord Baden Powell.
6. Jerome K Jerome.
7. 'Spy' (Sir Leslie Ward).
8. Sir Rufus Isaacs, Marquess of Reading.
9. Sir C Aubrey Smith.
Also, 10, an attempt by the author.

MARCOS, Ferdinand b. 1917. President of the Philippines, 1965–.

MARIA THERESA, 1717–80. Empress. Ruler of the Holy Roman Empire, Archduchess of Austria and Queen of Hungary and Bohemia. An important, though not rare, historical autograph.

MARIE ANTOINETTE, 1755–93. The luckless Queen of **Louis XVI** of France. Guillotined. Her autograph varied drastically. This example is from the British Museum.

MARIE LOUISE, 1791–1847. Empress. Second wife of **Napoleon**. A Princess of Austria.
A typical example of her tiny autograph.

MARIE de MEDICI, 1573–1642. Queen. Consort of **Henry IV** of France. Regent during the minority of their son **Louis XIII**.

MARLBOROUGH, John Churchill, Duke of 1650–1722. One of the greatest soldiers in Britain's history. Victor of Blenheim, Ramillies and Malplaquet in the War of the Spanish Succession.

MARLOWE, Christopher 1564–93. English dramatist and poet (*Dr Faustus*, etc.). Until fairly recently not a single word in Marlowe's hand was known to have survived. This unique signature, the third of those shown, the others being his father, uncle and brother, is as witness to a Will of 1583. (Kent County Archives.)

MARMONT, Auguste F L V de, Duc de Raguse 1774–1852. Marshal of the French Empire. His renunciation of Napoleon has earned him permanent notoriety. See also with Napoleonic Marshals page 179.

MARSHALL, George Catlett 1880–1959. American soldier and statesman. Army Chief of Staff in World War II. As Secretary of State thereafter, initiated the 'Marshall Plan' of giving American aid to Europe.

MARTIN, Frank 1890–1974. Swiss composer of oratorio *Golgotha*, cantata *Le Vin herbé*, etc.
Autograph musical extract from his Concerto for Cello. Reproduced by permission of Mrs Frank Martin. (Author's Collection.)

MARX, Karl 1818–83. German political philosopher. Regarded as the founder of modern communism. A much sought-after autograph.

MARY I, 1516–58. 'Bloody Mary' Tudor. Daughter of **Henry VIII** and **Catherine of Aragon**. Queen of England 1553–8.
Document in English addressed to the Master of the Great Wardrobe, Sir Edward Waldegrave who has signed as receiving it (bottom right). Orders for the making of a uniform for the Royal Plumber. This includes a coat to be made of three yards of red cloth with the Royal Cypher 'M.R.' embroidered on both the breast and back.
Signed 'Marye the Quene', Westminster, 20 June 1557. (Author's Collection.)

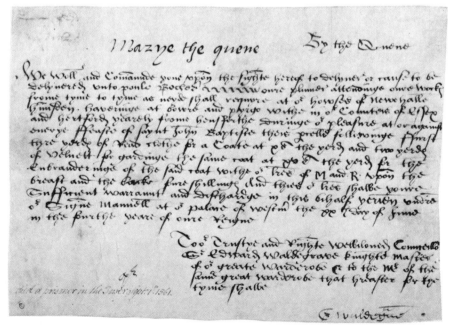

MARY II, 1662–94. British Queen. Ruled jointly with her husband **William III**.
Scarce signature. See also with British Sovereigns page 25.

MARY QUEEN of SCOTS 1542–87. The luckless Mary Stuart. Daughter of **James V** of Scotland. Queen of **Francis II** of France. Imprisoned for nineteen years by her cousin **Elizabeth I** and finally executed.

Her signature is above that of her mother Mary of Guise (1515–60) which is very similar. Confusion is added to by the fact that Mary of Guise signed Scottish documents on behalf of her daughter whilst Regent.

MASARYK, Thomas Garrigue 1850–1937. The founder and first President, 1918–35 of Czechoslovakia.

MASCAGNI, Pietro 1863–1945. Italian composer, famed for his opera *Cavalleria Rusticana*.

MASEFIELD, John 1878–1967. English man of letters. Poet Laureate. He is largely remembered as a poet of the sea.

MASOCH, Leopold von Sacher- 1836–95. German novelist. The word 'masochism' comes from the form of sexual eroticism featured in some of his novels.
See also with Dictionary Names page 110.

MASSÉNA, André, Prince of Essling 1758–1817. Perhaps the greatest of the Napoleonic Marshals.
See also with Napoleonic Marshals page 179.

MASSENET, Jules 1842–1912. French composer.
Autograph excerpt from the prelude to the fourth act of his opera *Hérodiade*. (Author's Collection.)

MATHER, Cotton 1663–1728. American Congregational theologian and educationalist.

Cotton Mather.

MATISSE, Henri 1869–1954. French painter. Leader of the Fauve school, he was influenced by the impressionists and cubists. A sought-after autograph.

MATTHEWS, Sir Stanley b. 1915. The first professional footballer to be knighted. He made 54 international appearances for England between 1935 and 1957.

MAUGHAM, W(illiam) Somerset 1874–1965. English author of *The Moon and Sixpence*, *Of Human Bondage*, etc.

MAUPASSANT, Guy de 1850–93. French author, famed for his short stories.

MAUROIS, André, pseudonym of Emile Herzog 1885–1967. French man of letters.

MAWSON, Sir Douglas 1882–1958. English-Australian Antarctic explorer and geologist.

MAXIM, Sir Hiram (S) 1840–1916. American-born, British inventor of the Maxim (machine) gun. He also patented a type of electric lamp and invented a type of flying machine in 1894.

MAXIMILIAN I, 1459–1519. Holy Roman Emperor 1493–1519. 'The Last of the Knights'.

MAXIMILIAN II, 1527–76. Holy Roman Emperor, 1564–76.

MAXIMILIAN, (Ferdinand Joseph) 1832–67. Emperor of Mexico. The unfortunate Austrian prince who, with French backing, assumed the throne of Mexico, 1864, only to be defeated by **Juarez** and shot.

MAYAKOVSKY, Vladimir V 1893–1930. Soviet futurist poet and satirical playwright.

MAZARIN, Jules 1602–61. French Cardinal-statesman. A successor to **Richelieu**, he was all-powerful during the minority of **Louis XIV**.

MAZZINI, Giuseppe 1805–72. Italian patriot. With **Cavour** and **Garibaldi** he accomplished the unification of Italy.

MEDICI, Cosimo de 1389–1464. Ruler of Florence, patron of the arts. Founder of the great Medici dynasty.

MEDICI, COSIMO I de 1519–74. 'The Great'. Duke of Florence and Grand-duke of Tuscany. A cruel but able ruler and patron of the arts. Signature in Italian as 'The Duke of Florence'.

MEDICI, Lorenzo de 1449–92. 'Lorenzo the Magnificent'. Ruler of Florence, patron of the arts. One of the outstanding historic figures of the Italian Renaissance.
An example of his scarce autograph together with a more studied signature in Latin.

MEDINA-SIDONIA, Alonso Pérez de Guzmán, Duke of 1550–1615. Spain's 'Admiral of the Ocean'. **Philip II**'s defeated commander of the Spanish Armada against England.

MEIR, Golda b. 1898. Russian-born Israeli stateswoman and Prime Minister 1969–74.

MELANCHTHON, originally Schwarzerd Philip 1497–1560. German religious reformer and humanist. Melanchthon is the Greek translation of his original surname meaning 'Black Earth'.

MELBA, Dame Nellie 1861–1931. Australian soprano prima donna. *Neé* Mitchell.

MELBOURNE, William Lamb, 2nd Viscount 1779–1848. Queen **Victoria**'s first Prime Minister.
See also with British Prime Ministers page 69.

MELVILLE, Herman 1819–91. American novelist famed for his classic *Moby Dick*.
A desirable American literary autograph.

MENDEL, Gregor Johann 1822–84. Austrian biologist. Propounded Mendel's Law of organic inheritance of character in plants and animals.

M

MENDELSSOHN (-BARTHOLDY), (J) (L) Felix 1809–47. German composer. Also distinguished as a pianist and organist. Variant autographs.

MENOTTI, Gian-Carlo b. 1911. American composer born in Italy. Writes his own libretti for his operas, such as *Amelia goes to the Ball*.

MENUHIN, Yehudi b. 1916. American violinist. Was a boy prodigy, first appearing in public as a soloist at the age of seven.

MENZIES, Sir Robert (Gordon) b. 1894. Australian statesman. Prime Minister, 1939–41 and 1949–66.

MERCATOR, Gerhardus, latinised form of Gerhard Kremer 1512–94. Flemish cartographer and mathematician. Produced the Mercator map projection.

MÉRIMÉE, Prosper 1803–70. French author of *Carmen* on which **Bizet** based his opera.

MESMER, Friedrich Anton or Franz 1734–1815. Austrian physician who developed the theory of animal magnetism now known as mesmerism.
See also under Dictionary Names page 110.

METAXAS, Yannis 1871–1941. Greek patriot, soldier and statesman. Prime Minister 1936–41.

METTERNICH, Prince Klemens W L von 1773–1859. Austrian statesman. For some 40 years he controlled his country's foreign policies.

MEYERBEER, Giacomo, originally Jakob Beer 1791–1864. German composer of French-style operas. His *Robert le Diable* is particularly outstanding.

MICHAEL I, b. 1921. Twice King of Rumania. Abdicated 1947.

MICHELANGELO (BUONARROTI), 1475–1564. Italian painter, sculptor, architect and poet. A major figure of the Renaissance and one of the greatest names in the history of art. His major sculptures include *David* in Florence and *Pietà* at St Peter's, Rome. He was responsible for the decoration in fresco style of the ceiling of the Sistine Chapel in the Vatican. A form of his autograph and a rare ALS. (The British Library.)

MICHELSON, Albert Abraham 1852–1931. Physicist. The first American to win a Nobel Prize, 1907. His Michelson-Morley experiment contributed to **Einstein**'s theory of relativity.

MIKOYAN, Anastas Ivanovich b. 1895. Soviet statesman. President of the USSR 1964–5.

MILHAUD, Darius 1892–1974. French composer. One-time leader of 'Les Six' group.

MILL, John Stuart 1806–73. Utilitarian philosopher, radical reformer and economist. Close associate of **Jeremy Bentham**.

MILLAIS, Sir John Everett 1829–96. English Pre-Raphaelite painter. His autograph and shortened signature together with a full signature.

MILLER, Arthur b. 1915. American playwright. *Death of a Salesman* and *The Crucible* are two of his major works. He was once married to the actress, Marilyn Monroe.

MILLER, Henry b. 1891. American author of such works as the formerly banned *Tropic of Cancer*.

MILLET, Jean François 1814–75. French painter. Painted scenes of country life, such as his masterpiece *The Sower*.

MILNE, A(lan) A(lexander) 1882–1956. English author. Known for his children's classics such as *Winnie-the-Pooh* and the collection of verse, *When We were Very Young*.

MILTON, John 1608–74. English poet and dramatist. Famed for his *Paradise Lost*, *Samson Agonistes* and *Lycidas*. Blind after 1652.
A rare literary autograph of major importance. Variant signatures in Latin and English.

MINTOFF, Dom(inic) b. 1916. Maltese Labour politician and Prime Minister.

MIRABEAU, Honoré Gabriel Riqueti, Comte de 1749–91. French orator, Revolutionary statesman and political essayist.

MIRÓ, Joán b. 1893. Spanish surrealist painter.
Signature as used on his paintings.

MISTRAL, Frédéric 1830–1914. French Provençal poet. His masterpiece was *Miréio*. Won Nobel Prize, 1904.

MIX, Tom 1880–1940. The cowboy hero star of the silent films. As adventurous in real life as on the screen, he fought in the Spanish American and Boer Wars, was a sheriff in Kansas and Oklahoma and served in the Texas Rangers.
PS. (Author's Collection.)

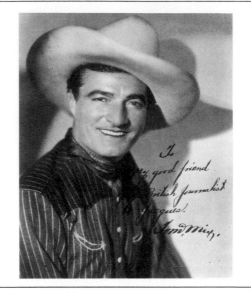

MODIGLIANI, Amedeo 1884–1920. Italian painter and sculptor. His portraits were characterised by their elongation.

MOHAMMED ALI, 1769–1849. 'Mehemet Ali', Viceroy of Egypt. Originally an Albanian officer, supported the Egyptians in their overthrow of the Mamelukes and rose to be ruler of his adopted country.

MOLIÈRE, pseudonym of Jean Baptiste Poquelin 1622–73. French dramatist. His many famous comedies include *Le Bourgeois Gentilhomme* and *Tartuffe*. A rare and important French literary autograph.

MOLOTOV, Vyacheslav M, formerly Skriabin b. 1890. Soviet statesman. Foreign Minister 1939–49. President of the Central Committee 1930–41. Notorious for his frequent use of the word 'No'!

Also see signature with **Stalin**.

MOLTKE, Helmuth, Count von 1800–91. Prussian Field-Marshal. Reorganised the Prussian Army, defeating Denmark, Austria and, in 1870, France.

MONCEY, Adrien J de, Duc de Conegliano 1754–1842. French soldier.
See also with Napoleonic Marshals page 179.

MONCK, George, Duke of Albemarle 1608–70. British soldier. Though he served Parliament as both a General and an Admiral in the Civil War, he brought about the restoration of **Charles II**.

MONET, Claude 1840–1926. French impressionist painter. Associated with **Sisley**, **Renoir** and **Pissarro**.

MONGKUT (RAMA IV), 1804–68. Enlightened King of Siam 1851–68. The book concerning his engagement of a British governess for his children, *Anna and the King of Siam*, became a highly successful musical play and film as *The King and I*.

MONMOUTH, James Scott, Duke of 1649 85. Illegitimate son of **Charles II**. Rebelled against **James II**.
An ANS pleading for intercession with the King six days before his execution. (The British Library.)

MONROE, James 1758–1831. Fifth President of the USA. Promulgated the 'Monroe Doctrine' of non-intervention by Europe in American affairs.
Also see with US Presidents page 204.

MONTAIGNE, Michel E de 1533–92. French man of letters, famed for his *Essays*.

MONTCALM (DE SAINT-VERAN), Louis Joseph, Marquis de 1712–59. Gallant French soldier defeated by **Wolfe** at Quebec where both commanders were mortally wounded.

MONTESQUIEU, Charles de Secondat, Baron de la Brède et de 1689–1755. French political philosopher and man of letters.

MONTEVERDI, Claudio G A 1567–1643. Italian composer. A scarce musical signature.

MONTEZ, Lola. Stage name of Maria Gilbert 1818–61. Irish dancer and adventuress. As mistress of **Ludwig I** of Bavaria, she became Countess of Landsfeld.

MONTGOLFIER, Joseph Michel 1740–1810 and (Jacques) Étienne 1745–99. French aeronauts who constructed the first successful balloon which flew 6 miles at 300 feet, 1783.

MONTGOMERY (OF ALAMEIN), Bernard Law, Viscount 1887–1976 'Monty'. British Field Marshal who drove the Germans from North Africa in World War II and as Commander, Allied Armies received the German surrender on Luneburg Heath.

MOORE, George 1852–1933. Irish man of letters. Associated with **Yeats** in the setting up of the Abbey Theatre, Dublin.

MOORE, Henry (S) b. 1898. British sculptor. One of his best-known works is *Madonna and Child* in St Matthew's Church, Northampton.

MOORE, Sir John 1761–1809. British General. Killed at Coruña in the Peninsular War. The subject of Wolfe's poem 'The Burial of Sir John Moore'.

MOORE, Thomas 1779–1852. Irish poet. 'The Bard of Erin'. His greatest work is perhaps *Lalla Rookh*.

MORE, Sir Thomas. Saint Thomas More 1478–1535. English saint, statesman, scholar and writer. One of the most outstanding figures of British history, the author of *Utopia* and Lord Chancellor. Beheaded as the result of refusing to accept the King, **Henry VIII**, as sole head of the Church and to agree to his divorce from **Catherine of Aragon**. Canonised 1935.

MORGAN, John Pierpont 1837–1913. American multi-millionaire banker, financier and philanthropist.
The signature only is in his hand.

MORRIS, William 1834–96. English poet, philosopher, artist, craftsman and socialist. ALS explaining that he has only written one sonnet in his life, 21 July 1880. (Author's Collection.)

MORSE, Samuel F B 1791–1872. American inventor of an electric telegraph and of the universal system of telegraphic communication, the Morse Code.

MORTIER, Édouard A C J, Duc de Trevise 1768–1835. French Marshal. See also with Napoleonic Marshals page 179.

M

MOUNTBATTEN OF BURMA, Louis F A V N, Earl, b. 1900. British Naval Officer. Supreme Allied Commander, S E Asia, 1943–6. Last Viceroy and First Governor General of India.

MOZART, Wolfgang Amadeus 1756–91. Austrian composer. Famed for his instrumental music, he was also responsible for the operas *The Marriage of Figaro*, *Don Giovanni* and *The Magic Flute*.
Two examples of his scarce and highly important autograph, in italic and German script.
Also autograph music at British Library.

MUNTHE, Axel 1857–1949. Swedish-born, British naturalised author of the modern classic *The Story of San Michele*.

MURAT, Joachim 1767–1815. French Marshal. Brother-in-law of **Napoleon** and, as Joachim I Napoleon, King of Naples 1808–15. See also with Napoleonic Marshals page 179.

MURILLO, Bartolomé Esteban 1617–82. Spanish painter. Founded the academy at Seville.

MUSSET, (L) (C) Alfred de 1810–57. French poet, dramatist and novelist. He was one of **George Sand**'s numerous lovers.

MUSSOLINI, Benito 1883–1945. 'Il Duce', Italian dictator. Founder of the Fascist Party. Prime Minister 1922–43.

NABOKOV, Vladimir 1899–1977 Russian-born American novelist. Wrote *Lolita*, etc. The opening lines of the autograph manuscript of his novel *Ada*. This extract supplied by Mrs Nabokov and reproduced by kind permission of Mr Nabokov.

Ada, a novel
MS §1 ①

"All happy families are more or less dissimilar; all unhappy ones are more or less alike," says a great Russian writer in the beginning of a famous novel (Anna Arkadievitch Karenina, transfigured into English by R.G. Stonelower, Mount Tabor Ltd, 1880). That pronouncement has little if any relation to the story to be unfolded now, a family chronicle, the first part of which is, perhaps, closer to another Tolstoy work, Detstvo i Otrochestvo (Childhood and Fatherland, Pontius Press, 1858).

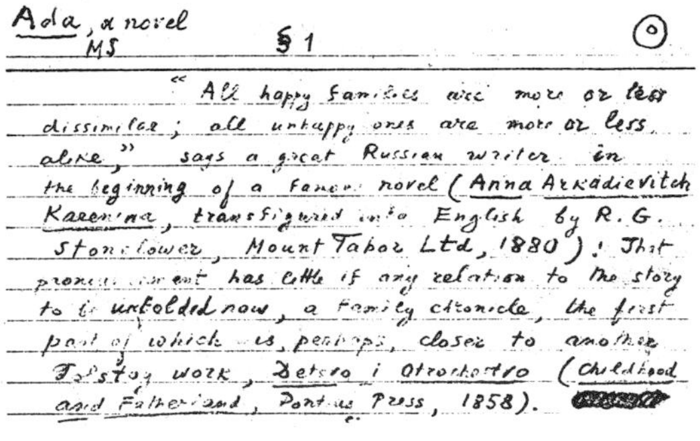

NANSEN, Fridtjof 1861–1930. Norwegian Arctic explorer, scientist and diplomat. Reached the then furthest point north, 1895. Winner of the 1922 Nobel Peace Prize for work for post-war refugees.

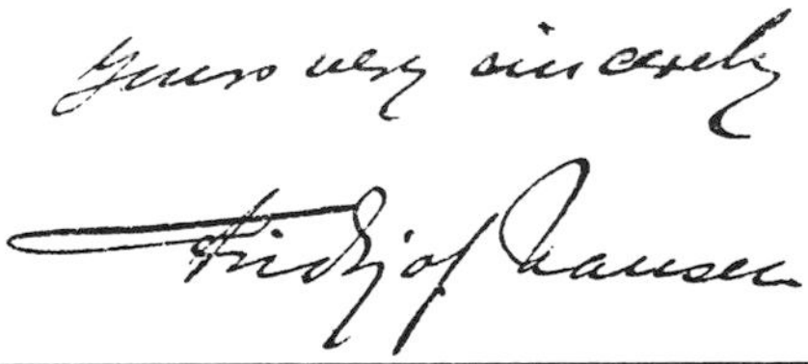

NAPOLEON I, Bonaparte formerly Buonaparte 1769–1821. Emperor of the French. France's greatest military genius. Because his name is one of the most famous in world history, Napoleon's autograph, though not yet scarce, is greatly sought after. Napoleon signed in many ways, firstly, 'Buonaparte', then 'Bonaparte' when First Consul and 'N', 'Np', 'Npl' and 'Napol' as Emperor. He signed his full name only infrequently. A selection of his signatures are shown here. The last is from his will at St Helena. It would be possible to reproduce 500 genuine signatures of Napoleon all of which would be at variance with each other. Also DS with his typical large 'N'. (Author's Collection.)

A Sa Majesté l'Empereur et Roi.
Bureau
Du 1. Décembre 1811

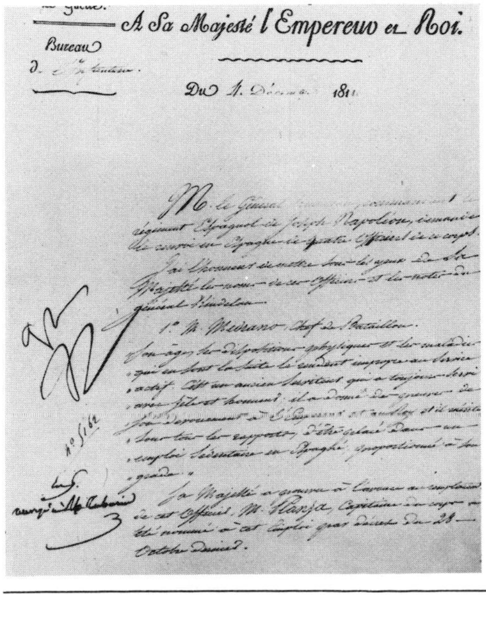

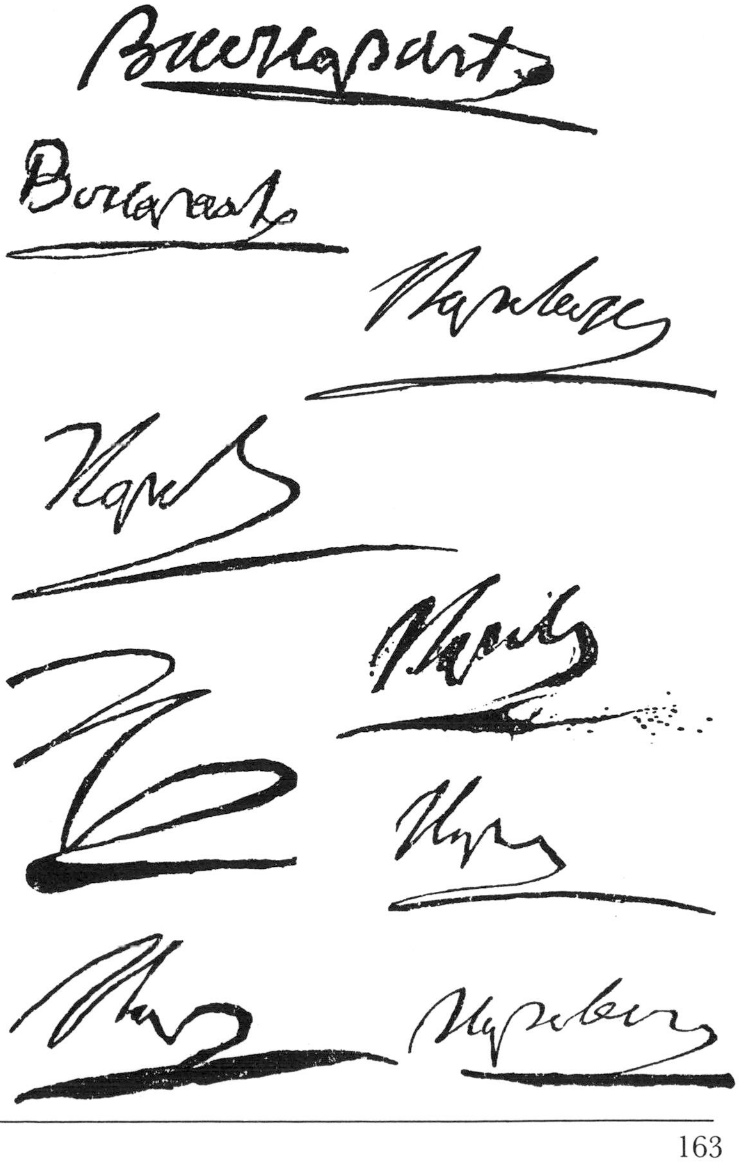

N

NAPOLEON II, François C J Bonaparte, Duke of Reichstadt 1811–32. King of Rome. **Napoleon**'s only legitimate son, by **Marie Louise**. Nicknamed 'L'Aiglon' – the Eaglet. His signature shown here is very rare. His short life makes his autograph scarce in any form and this is mostly found in extracts from his school exercise books.

NAPOLEON III, (Charles) Louis Napoleon Bonaparte 1808–73. Emperor of the French 1852–70. Nephew of **Napoleon I**.

NASH, John 1752–1835. The English Regency architect. Designed Regent's Park and its approaches.

NASH, Ogden 1902–71. American humorist and poet.

NASSER, Gamal Abdel 1918–70. Egyptian statesman. President 1954–70.
His signature in English and Egyptian.

NECKER, Jacques 1732–1804. French statesman.
Note the typical difference in the size of his signature and handwriting.

NEHRU, Jawaharlal 1889–1964. Indian statesman. First Prime Minister, 1947–64. In the course of his lifelong struggle to achieve independence for his country, he spent 18 years in gaol.

NELSON, Horatio, Viscount 1758–1805. Britain's greatest naval hero. The victor of the Nile and Trafalgar. Examples of his signature, (1) with his right hand before losing that arm in 1797, in which form his autograph is scarce, and (2) with his left hand, which includes his Sicilian title of Duke of Bronte.
Also the first page of his last unfinished letter. (The British Library.)

1.

2.

NEWCASTLE, Thomas Pelham-Holles, Duke of 1693–1768. English statesman.
See also with British Prime Ministers page 68.

NEWMAN, John Henry 1801–90. English cardinal, theologian and Church reformer.
Signature and part ALS.

NEWTON, Sir Isaac 1642–1727. English natural philosopher and mathematician. Set out the law of gravitation and developed differential calculus independently of **Leibniz**.
Variant examples of his signature.

NEY, Michel, Prince de La Moskova 1769–1815. One of the most colourful Marshals of Napoleon.
See also with Napoleonic Marshals page 179.

NICHOLAS I, 1796–1855. Tsar of Russia 1825–55.
Signature as Russian.

NICHOLAS II, 1868–1918. Tsar of Russia 1894–1917. Shot with his whole family after the Revolution.
His signature in Roman and Russian script.

NICKLAUS, Jack (W) b. 1940. American golfer. Winner of many major golf titles, including US Masters a record five times, US Open three times and British Open twice. Top money winner in golfing history.

NIEMOLLER, Martin b. 1892. German Lutheran pastor and defiant anti-Nazi. An ace U-boat commander in World War I, he suffered imprisonment in concentration camps for his opposition to **Hitler**'s regime.

NIEPCE, Joseph Nicéphore 1765–1833. French chemist and physicist. One of the inventors of photography.

NIETZSCHE, Friedrich Wilhelm 1844–1900. German philosopher, critic and poet.

NIGHTINGALE, Florence 1820–1910. English nurse and hospital reformer. 'The Lady with the Lamp' who organised the military hospitals in the Crimea. Florence Nightingale wrote frequently in pencil and it will be seen from these examples that her pencilled autograph was more or less upright, whereas when in ink her handwriting was sloped.

NIJINSKY, Waslav 1890–1950. Russian ballet dancer. Joined the Ballets Russes of **Diaghilev**, 1909. The most famous male dancer of all time, he became insane at the age of 27, so that his autograph is scarce.

NIMITZ, Chester (William) 1885–1966. American Admiral. C-in-C the Pacific Fleet in World War II and Chief of Naval Operations thereafter.

NIXON, Richard Milhous b. 1913. President of the USA 1969–74. Also see with US Presidents page 205.

NKRUMAH, Kwame 1909–72. African nationalist leader. Prime Minister of the Gold Coast (Ghana) on its independence, 1957 and first President of Ghana 1960–6.

NOBEL, Alfred Bernhard 1833–96. Swedish chemist, manufacturer and philanthropist. The discoverer of dynamite. Instigated and provided funds for the Nobel prizes.

NORTH, Frederick, Lord, 2nd Earl of Guilford 1732–92. British Prime Minister at the time of the American War of Independence. See also with British Prime Ministers page 68.

NOSTRADAMUS, Latinised name of Michel de Notre-dame 1503–66. French astrologer and physician whose predictions of the future, expressed in symbolic rhyme, brought him lasting fame. A rare autograph.

NUFFIELD, William R Morris, Viscount 1877–1963. British motor-car manufacturer and philanthropist. Founded Nuffield College, Oxford and the Nuffield Foundation for research.

NUREYEV, Rudolph (Hametovich) b. 1939. Russian-born ballet dancer. Famed for his partnership with **Margot Fonteyn**.

NURMI, Paavo (Johannes) 1897–1973. Finnish athlete who won a world record twelve Olympic medals (nine gold, three silver).

NYERERE, Julius Kambarage b. 1922. Tanganyikan nationalist statesman. First Prime Minister and, in 1962, first President of Tanganyika, he continued in that office when his country was united with Zanzibar as Tanzania, 1964. PS. (Author's Collection.)

OAKLEY, Annie, Phoebe Anne Oakley Mozee Butler 1860–1926. American markswoman. The subject of the musical play *Annie Get your Gun*. For seventeen years with the circus run by 'Buffalo Bill' **Cody**; she once shot a cigarette out of the Kaiser's mouth; at his request one should add! Signed card. (M H Loewenstern Collection, Amarillo, Texas.)

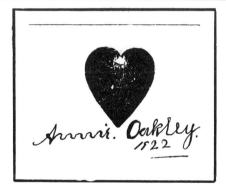

O'CASEY. Sean 1884–1964. Irish playwright. Wrote *Juno and the Paycock* and *Shadow of a Gunman*.

O'CONNELL, Daniel 1775–1847. Irish nationalist leader and patriot. 'The Liberator' who, subsequent to the Catholic Emancipation Act, entered the British Parliament, 1829.

OFFENBACH, Jacques 1819–80. Jewish German-born French composer of operas *Orpheus in the Underworld*, *Tales of Hoffman*, etc. Also known for the music to which the Can-Can is danced.

OHM, Georg Simon 1787–1854. German physicist. Propounded Ohm's Law of electrical currents. The electrical resistance unit, the ohm, is named after him.

OLAV V, b. 1903. King of Norway 1957–. Son of **Haakon VII** and of Maud, daughter of **Edward VII**, he was born in England.

OLIVARES, Gaspar de Guzmán, El Conde-Duque de 1587–1645. Spanish states-man. Chief Minister of **Philip IV**. Variant signatures as 'El Conde-Duque' and 'El Conde de Olivares'.

OLIVIER, Laurence (Kerr), Lord b. 1907. British actor and theatrical director. The first actor to receive a peerage.

O'NEILL, Eugene (Gladstone) 1888–1953. American dramatist of *Mourning Becomes Electra* and *Long Day's Journey into Night* fame. Won Nobel Prize, 1936.

ORCZY, Baroness Emmuska 1865–1947. Hungarian-born British adventure writer. Created the Scarlet Pimpernel.

ORWELL, George pseudonym of Eric Arthur Blair 1903–50. Novelist and essayist famous for his satirical novels *Animal Farm* (1945) and *Nineteen Eighty-four* (1949) in which he expresses his mistrust of all political parties.

OSBORNE, John (James) b. 1929. British dramatist. Wrote *Look Back in Anger* and *The Entertainer*.

OSLER, Sir William 1849–1919. Canadian physician noted for work on angina pectoris and blood and spleen diseases.

OTTO I, 'The Great' 912–73. King of Germany and, 962–73, Holy Roman Emperor.

An example of his excessively rare holograph *signum* in the form of a monogram of his name from a grant to a monastery, dated 941.

OTTO III, 980–1002. Holy Roman Emperor. Grandson of **Otto I**, 'The Great', he succeeded his father, Otto II, at the age of three. He lived much of his very short life in Rome and died in Paterno.

His very rare monogram, the crossbar of which is autograph, from a Church document, Ravenna, 1 December 1001.

OUDINOT, Nicolas Charles, Duc de Reggio 1767–1847. The most battle-scarred – 'The Marshal of the Thirty-four Wounds' – of **Napoleon**'s Marshals. See also with Napoleonic Marshals page 179.

OWEN, Sir Richard 1804–92. British zoologist and anatomist.

OWEN, Robert 1771–1858. Welsh social reformer. Pioneer of the co-operative movement.

OWENS, Jesse b. 1913. American athlete. Set six World Records in one day, 25 May 1935.

PAASIKIVI, Juo Kusti 1870–1956. Finnish statesman. Prime Minister and President 1946–56.

PADEREWSKI, Ignace Jan 1860–1941. Polish pianist, composer and statesman. Prime Minister of Poland 1919.

PAGANINI, Nicolo 1782–1840. Italian virtuoso violinist. Paganini's scarce autograph is more in demand than that of any other instrumentalist.

PAHLAVI, Mohammed Reza b. 1919. The Shahanshah Aryamehr. Ruler of Iran 1941–.

PAINE, Thomas 1737–1809. British-born American radical philosopher. Wrote *The Rights of Man* and supported the French Revolution.

PALAFOX (y **MELZI**) José de, Duke of Saragossa 1780–1847. Spanish soldier. Successful defender of Saragossa 1808–9.

PALESTRINA, Giovanni Pierluigi da 1525–94. Italian composer and papal choirmaster.
Signature and an example of his excessively rare musical autograph from the *Codek 59*. (St John Lateran archives.)

PALLADIO, Andrea 1518–80. Italian architect who founded modern architecture. He adapted the Roman principles, later to be referred to as the Palladian style.

P

PALMER, Arnold b. 1929. American golfer. He has won all the major Golf Championship titles.

PALMERSTON, Henry John Temple, 3rd Viscount 1784–1865. A distinguished Foreign Minister, he was also twice Prime Minister of Britain. See also with British Prime Ministers page 69.

PAPEN, Franz von 1879–1969. German Chancellor before **Hitler**; and his deputy thereafter.

PARK, Mungo 1771–1806. Scottish explorer of the Niger. He was drowned in that river after being attacked by natives in his canoe.

PARNELL, Charles Stewart 1846–91. Irish nationalist leader who fought for Home Rule.

PARRY, Sir William (Edward) 1790–1855. English Admiral and Arctic explorer who searched for the Northwest Passage.

PASCAL, Blaise 1623–62. French philosopher, scientist, mathematician and man of letters. The author of *Pensées*.
A very rare and important literary autograph.

PASTERNAK, Boris (Leonidovich) 1890–1960. Russian poet and novelist famed for *Dr Zhivago*.

PASTEUR, Louis 1822–95. French chemist. Developed pasteurisation, by part sterilisation of milk and vaccines to combat hydrophobia, rabies, anthrax and cholera.

PATON, Alan (Stewart) b. 1903. South African author of *Cry, the Beloved Country*. See PS with others under **Roy Campbell** page 35.

PATTI, Adelina 1843–1919. Italian operatic coloratura soprano.
Signature as Baroness Cederström.

PATTON, George Smith 1885–1945. 'Blood and Guts' Patton, American soldier. Commanded the victorious 3rd Army in Western Europe, World War II.
Though modern, his autograph is scarce.

PAUL I, 1754–1801. Tsar of Russia 1796–1801. Son of **Catherine the Great**.

PAUL VI, Pope Giovanni Battista Montini b. 1897. The 263rd Pontiff of the Church of Rome from 1963.
Signature when Archbishop of Milan.

PAULING, Linus Carl b. 1901. American chemist and worker for peace. The first individual ever to win two Nobel prizes outright – for Chemistry, 1954 and Peace, 1962.

PAVLOVA, Anna 1885–1931. Russian ballerina. Renowned for her role in *The Dying Swan*.
PS. (Author's Collection.)

PEARSON, Lester (Bowles) 1897–1972. Canadian Prime Minister 1963–8. Won Nobel Peace Prize, 1957.

PEARY, Robert 1856–1920. American Admiral and Arctic explorer. Accepted popularly as the first man to reach the North Pole, 1909. Some authorities dispute this, mainly on the grounds that it seems unlikely that he could have covered certain distances involved in the time claimed. None, however, will doubt his heroic efforts to achieve his end, involving four expeditions and lasting nearly sixteen years.

PEDRO II, 1825–91. Last Emperor of Brazil 1831–89. A progressive ruler, he nonetheless had to abdicate to make way for a republic.

PEEL, Sir Robert 1788–1850. British Prime Minister.
See also with British Prime Ministers page 69.

PELÉ, properly Edson Arantes do Nascimento b. 1940. Brazilian footballer. A great exponent of the game, he led his country three times to World Cup victories.

PELHAM, Henry *c.* 1695–1754. British Prime Minister.
See also with British Prime Ministers page 68.

PENN, William 1644–1718. English Quaker founder of Pennsylvania. Laid out the city of Philadelphia.

PÉPIN III, 'The Short' *c.* 714–768. King of the Franks and of Germany. Father of **Charlemagne** and founder of the Carolingian dynasty of Holy Roman Emperors (of the West). His extremely rare attested *signum.*

PEPYS, Samuel 1633–1703. English diarist. Pepys' signature can sometimes be found on Naval documents as he was Secretary of the Admiralty under **Charles II**.

PERAL (y CABALLERO), Isaac 1851–95. Spanish submarine inventor.

PERCIVAL, Spencer 1762–1812. The only British Prime Minister to have been assassinated.
See also with British Prime Ministers page 68.

PERIGNON, Dominique C, Marquis de 1756–1818. French Marshal of the Empire. See also with Napoleonic Marshals page 179.

PERÓN, Juan Domingo 1895–1974. Argentinian dictator. President 1946–1955. Re-elected 1973. His first wife Eva (1919–52) became a powerful influence politically and his second wife succeeded as President on his death.

PERRY, Fred(erick) (John) b. 1909. English tennis player. Won three successive Wimbledon Singles Championships 1934–6.

PERSHING, John J(oseph) 1860–1948. American General. C-in-C, American Forces in World War I.

PESTALOZZI, Johann Heinrich 1746–1827. Swiss educational reformer. Variant examples of his autograph.

PÉTAIN, Henri Philippe 1856–1951. French Marshal. A courageous defender of Verdun in World War I, he became Premier of the Vichy Government of France in World War II and ended his life, disgraced and imprisoned for collaboration with the enemy.

PETER I, 'The Great' 1672–1725. Tsar of Russia 1682–1725. Raised Russia to a position of power in Europe. A royal autograph of major importance.

PETRARCH, Francesco Petrarca 1304–74. Italian Renaissance poet and humanist. An example of his usual handwriting and a more studied and careful extract from an autograph manuscript in the Vatican Library. A rare and important literary autograph.

PHILIP II, 1527–98. King of Spain 1556–98. His second wife was 'Bloody' **Mary I**. A fanatic Roman Catholic, he reinstated the dreaded Inquisition and sent the ill-fated Spanish Armada against England. Signature as 'Yo el Rey' ('I the King').

PHILIP IV, 1605–65. King of Spain 1621–65.
Signature as 'Yo el Rey' ('I the King'). All Kings of Spain signed official letters and documents in this fashion.

PHILIP, Prince, Duke of Edinburgh b. 1921. Consort of Queen Elizabeth II whom he married in 1947. Son of Prince Andrew of Greece.

PHILLPOTTS, Eden 1862–1960. English novelist, dramatist and poet who produced over 250 works.

PIAF, Edith. Edith Giovanna Gassion 1915–63. French singer, known as 'the Little Sparrow'.

PICASSO, Pablo Ruiz y, 1881–1973. Spanish post-impressionist painter and pioneer of cubism. A dominating figure in 20th-century art, his autograph is highly sought after.
Variant examples.

PICCARD, Auguste 1884–1962. Swiss physicist who explored the stratosphere by balloon and the ocean depths by bathyscope constructed by himself.

PICKFORD, Mary, stage name of Gladys Smith b. 1893. American film actress. Known as 'America's Sweetheart'.

The Marshals of the Napoleonic Empire

The Marshals created by Napoleon formed the most colourful body of military commanders in history. A motley band of regular soldiers and inspired amateurs – one had been an actor, another a barrel-cooper, yet a third a prince – they were a legend in their time, much respected by their enemies.

All twenty-six are shown here, identified only by their family surnames. For their many titles and biographical details see the individual entries in the main text.

Lannes

Berthier

Masséna

Poniatowski

The Marshals are:

1. Augereau.
2. Berthier, signed 'Alexandre' as Prince.
3. Bernadotte.
4. Bessières.
5. Brune.
6. Davout, signed as 'Prince d'Eckmuhl'.
7. Gouvion St Cyr.
8. Grouchy.
9. Jourdan.
10. Kellermann.
11. Lannes.
12. Lefebvre.
13. Macdonald.
14. Masséna.
15. Marmont.
16. Moncey.
17. Mortier.
18. Murat.
19. Ney.
20. Ouidinot.
21. Pérignon.
22. Poniatowski; the most scarce autographically.
23. Sérurier.
24. Soult, signed as 'Duc de Dalmatie'.
25. Suchet.
26. Victor.

All from documents and letters in the Author's Collection.

PIERCE, Franklin 1804–69. Fourteenth President of the USA 1853–7. See also with US Presidents page 204.

PIGGOTT, Lester (Keith) b. 1935. British champion jockey. Eight times winner of the Derby between 1954 and 1977.

PILATRE de ROZIER, Jean François 1756–85. French aeronaut. First human being to make a balloon ascent, 1785. Pilatre's autograph is of considerable rarity because of his early death when trying to cross the English Channel by balloon.

PINTER, Harold b. 1930. British dramatist. Works include *The Caretaker* and *The Homecoming*.

PIRANDELLO, Luigi 1867–1936. Italian dramatist, novelist and short-story writer. The leading playwright of the 'grotesque' school. Won Nobel Literature Prize, 1934.

PISSARRO, Camille 1830–1903. French impressionist painter. An associate of **Monet** and **Renoir**.

PITT, William, the Elder. Earl of Chatham 1708–78. 'The Great Commoner'. One of the most distinguished statesman in British history. See also with British Prime Ministers page 68.

PITT, William, The Younger 1759–1806. England's youngest and perhaps greatest Prime Minister. See also with other British Prime Ministers page 68.

PIUS VII, Pope. Luigi Barnaba Chiaramonti 1742–1823. The 252nd Pontiff 1800–23. Went to France to crown **Napoleon**.

PIUS IX, Pope. Giovanni M M Ferretti 1792–1878. The Pope, 1846–78, who proclaimed the dogma of the Immaculate Conception and whose Vatican Council formulated the dogma of Papal Infallibility.

PIZARRO, Francisco c. 1478–1541. Spanish 'Conquistador'. Conquered Peru and founded its capital, Lima.
A rare Spanish autograph.

PLANCK, Max (K E L) 1858–1947. German physicist. Won Nobel Prize, 1918 for the formulation of the quantum theory.

PLAYER, Gary b. 1936. South African golfer. Has won all the major championship titles.

PLIMSOLL, Samuel 1824–98. English shipping reformer. Responsible for the introduction of the legal load safety line on ships – the Plimsoll Line (Mark).

PLOMER, William (C F) b. 1903. British writer born in South Africa.

PODGORNY, Nikolay Viktorovich b. 1903. President of the USSR 1965–77.
As are most Soviet autographs, his signature is scarce.

POE, Edgar Allan 1809–49. American poet and short-story writer. A master of the macabre and suspense. His poetical masterpiece was 'The Raven'. An extrovert example of this scarce signature.

P

POINCARÉ, Raymond N L 1860–1934. President throughout World War I and thrice Prime Minister of France.

POLE, Reginald 1500–58. English cardinal. A cousin of **Henry VIII** and Archbishop of Canterbury under his Catholic daughter **Mary I**.
Variant signatures as 'Pole' and as Archbishop of Canterbury – 'Cantuarion'.
See connected DS by **Henry VIII** page 103.

POLK, James Knox 1795–1849. Eleventh President of the USA.
See also with US Presidents page 204.

POMBAL, Sebastião Jose(ph) de Carvalho e Melo Marquês de 1699–1782. Portuguese statesman. During Joseph Emanuel's reign he was the virtual ruler of Portugal. Variant signatures, in his own name and as Marquês.

POMPADOUR, Jeanne Antoinette Poisson, Marquise de 1721–64. 'Madame de Pompadour', all-powerful mistress of **Louis XV** of France.

POMPIDOU, Georges (J R) 1911–74. French President 1969–74, in succession to **De Gaulle**.

PONIATOWSKI, Prince Jozef Antoni 1762–1813. Polish soldier in the French Army. Poniatowski's signature, the most rare of all the Napoleonic Marshals, is also with those of his colleagues page 179.

182

POPE, Alexander 1688–1744. English poet and satirist.
An example of the much sought-after autograph of the author of *Essay on Criticism*, *The Rape of the Lock* and *The Dunciad*.

you in that hope, and return home full of acknowledgments for the Favors your Lordship has done me,

A. Pope.

PORTLAND, William H Cavendish-Bentinck, Duke of 1738–1809. British Prime Minister.
See also with British Prime Ministers page 68.

POTEMKIN, Prince Grigori A 1739–91. Russian Field Marshal, statesman and favourite of **Catharine (II)** The Great.

POTTER, (Helen) Beatrix 1866–1943. English authoress and illustrator of such children's classics as *The Tale of Peter Rabbit*. The last page of an illustrated holograph letter.
From *The Tale of Beatrix Potter* by Margaret Lane. By kind permission of the publishers, Frederick Warne & Co. Ltd.

but Flopsy, Mopsy, and Cottontail had bread and milk and blackberries for supper.   I am coming back to London next Thursday, so I hope I shall see you soon, and the new baby   I remain, dear Noel, yours affectionately Beatrix Potter

---

POULENC, Francis 1899–1963. French composer. One of 'Les Six' group.
Signed 'pin' sketch of himself at the piano. (Author's Collection.)

Francis Poulenc

London –

POUND, Ezra (Loomis) 1885–1973. A major, if controversial and eccentric, American poet and critic. His scarce, extrovert 'signature' consists here of part of his Christian name 'Ez' in the form of a face.

POUSSIN, Nicolas 1594–1665. French classic painter.
Often signed in the Italian form 'Nicolo' as shown here.

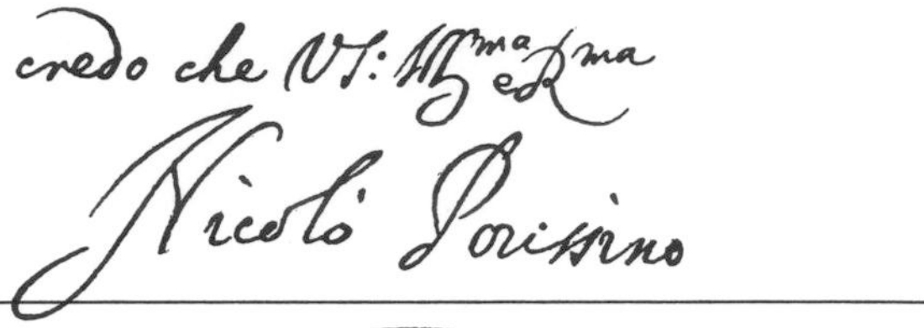

PRESLEY, Elvis (Aaron) 1935–77. American popular singer and film actor. Sales of his records are believed to have reached more than 200,000,000.

PRESS, Tamara b. 1937. Soviet Olympic shot putt and discus champion. Won both events in 1964 and the shot only in 1960.

PRÉVOST (d'EXILES), Abbé Antoine François 1697–1763. French adventurer and soldier turned priest and novelist. Author of *Manon Lescaut*.

PRIESTLEY, J(ohn) B(oynton) b. 1894. English novelist, playwright and critic. Author of *The Good Companions*, *Angel Pavement*, etc.

PRIESTLEY, Joseph 1733–1804. English chemist and theologian. A discoverer of oxygen.

PROKOFIEFF, Sergei S 1891–1953. Russian composer of *Peter and the Wolf*, etc.

PROTOPOPOV, Oleg b. 1932. Russian ice skater. With **Ludmilla Belousova**, World Pairs Champions 1965 to 1968, and Olympic Champions in 1964 and 1968.

PROUDHON, Pierre Joseph 1809–65. French socialist and Revolutionary writer. 'The Father of Anarchy'.

PROUST, Marcel 1871–1922. French novelist. Wrote the 13-volume novel *À la Recherche du Temps Perdu*.

PRUD'HON, Pierre Paul 1758–1823. French painter and interior designer. Executed a portrait of **Napoleon**'s first Empress, **Josephine**.

PUCCINI, Giacomo 1858–1924. Italian opera composer of *La Tosca*, *La Bohème*, etc. Signed autograph music extract from *Madame Butterfly*.
Puccini's autograph, particularly in the form of holograph music, though not yet scarce, is eagerly sought after.

PUGIN, Augustus W N 1812–52. English architect. A leading Gothic revivalist.

PURCELL, Henry 1659–95. English composer and organist.
His shaky signature on his will.

PUSHKIN, Aleksandr S 1799–1837. Russian poet known for *Eugene Onegin* and *Boris Godunov*.
Examples in Russian and italic script.

Q-R

QUASIMODO, Salvatore 1901–68. Patriotic Italian poet. Won Nobel Literature Prize, 1959.

RABELAIS, François *c*. 1494–1553. French satirist whose bawdy, riotous, yet witty and philosophical works have added the word 'rabelaisian' to the English dictionary. *Pantegruel* and *Gargantua* are his masterpieces.
Variant examples of his rare autograph.

RACHEL, stage name of Élisa Félix 1820–58. French tragic actress.

RACHMANINOFF, Sergei W 1873–1943. Russian composer and pianist. The Prelude in C sharp minor was one of his most popular works.

RACINE, Jean (B) 1639–99. French dramatist, famed for his tragedies *Andromaque*, *Phèdre*, etc.
A very rare autograph.

RACKHAM, Arthur 1867–1939. British artist and illustrator, particularly of fairy tales.

RADEK, Karl, formerly Sobelsohn 1885–1939? Polish-Russian Communist leader and journalist. A victim of **Stalin**'s purges, he is presumed to have died in prison.

RADETSKY, Joseph, Count 1766–1858. Austrian Field Marshal. Fought against **Napoleon** and Sardinia. The *Radetsky March* was written by **Johann Straus**, senior in his honour.

RADHAKRISHNAN, (Sir) Sarvepalli 1888–1975. Indian scholar, philosopher and statesman. President 1962–7.

RAEBURN, Sir Henry 1756–1823. Scottish portrait painter. Sir **Walter Scott** and **Boswell** were amongst his many subjects.

RAHMAN (PUTRA), Tunku Abdul b. 1903. Malaysia's first Prime Minister 1963.

RAINIER III, Prince b. 1923. Ruler of Monaco.
PS with Princess Grace. (Photo by Picedi *Editions La Cigogne*, Author's Collection.)

RALEGH, RALEIGH in modern form, Sir Walter 1552–1618. English navigator, courtier and writer. Introduced potatoes and tobacco into England and tried to colonise Virginia.
Two very different examples, both from the British Museum.

R

RAMAN, Sir Chandrasekhara V 1888–1970. Indian physicist. Won Nobel Prize, 1930, for study of diffusion of light, 'The Raman effect'.

RAMSAY, Sir William 1852–1916. Scottish chemist. Won Nobel Prize, 1904. Discovered argon with **Rayleigh**; also helium and crypton.

RAMUZ, Charles 1878–1947. Swiss man of letters.

RANJITSINGHI, Prince 1872–1933. Maharajah of Nawanagar. Indian cricketer. Excelled as a batsman.

RAPHAEL, Raffaello Santi or Sanzio 1483–1520. Italian painter and architect. One of the great masters of the Italian Renaissance.

RASPUTIN, Grigori Efimovich 1871?–1916. Russian peasant monk and court favourite who wielded a strange power over the Tsar **Nicholas II** and his consort. Murdered by noblemen led by Prince Yusupov.
A rare signature as 'Grigori' and a hurried ANS as 'Rasputin'.

RAVEL, Maurice 1875–1937. French composer.
Autographically much in demand, he is more known to the uninitiated for his popular lesser work *Bolero* than for his many more noteworthy compositions.

RAYLEIGH, John W Strutt, 3rd Lord 1842–1919. English physicist. Discoverer, with **Ramsay**, of argon. His autograph must not be confused with that of his son, which is more regular and upright.

READE, Charles 1814–84. English novelist. Known for the classic *The Cloister and the Hearth*.

READING, Rufus D Isaacs, Marquess of 1860–1935. English statesman and lawyer. Served as Lord Chief Justice, Foreign Secretary and Viceroy of India.
See also pig drawn blindfold page 147.

RÉAUMUR, René A F de 1683–1757. French scientist. Improved steel and iron manufacture, invented the Réaumur thermometer and researched into natural history and metallurgy.

RÉCAMIER, Madame Jeanne Françoise J A 1777–1849. French beauty and wit whose salon was the meeting place of the great and brilliant of her day, particularly **Chateaubriand**.

REHAN, Ada 1860–1916. Irish-born American actress. Variant autographs.

REINECKE, Karl 1824–1910. German pianist and composer. Known in particular for his interpretation of the works of **Mozart**.

RÉJANE, Gabrielle 1856–1920. French actress. After **Sarah Bernhardt**, she is accepted as France's next most distinguished actress.

R

REMARQUE, Erich Maria 1898–1970. German novelist. Known for the classic war story *All Quiet on the Western Front*.

REMBRANDT (VAN RIJN), 1606–69. Dutch master painter. A scarce and highly important autograph.

RENOIR, (Pierre) Auguste 1841–1919. French impressionist painter. Two widely differing examples of his autograph.

RETZ (or RAIS), Gilles de Laval, Baron de 1404–40. French warrior who fought by the side of **Joan of Arc**. Committed atrocities on 150 children and was hanged. Reputed original of the 'Bluebeard' legend.

REVERE, Paul 1735–1818. American engraver and patriot. Known for his ride, immortalised by **Longfellow**, from Boston to Lexington to warn of the approach of the British.

REYNOLDS, Sir Joshua 1723–92. English portrait painter. First President of the Royal Academy, 1768.

RHEE, Syngman 1875–1965. Korean patriot and statesman. President 1948–60.

President of Republic of Korea.

RHODES, Cecil John 1853–1902. British administrator, financier and philanthropist in South Africa. Made a fortune on diamond mining from which he endowed the Rhodes scholarships at Oxford. Prime Minister of Cape Colony, 1890–6. Rhodesia was named after him. PS (Author's Collection) and variant autograph.

RICHARD II, 1367–1400. King of England 1377–99. Deposed by Bolingbroke (later **Henry IV**). Murdered in Pontefract Castle.
See also with British Sovereigns page 24.

RICHARD III, 'Crouchback' 1452–85. King of England 1483–5. Defeated (and killed) at Bosworth by Richmond (**Henry VII**). Signatures as Duke of Gloucester.
See also with British Sovereigns page 24.

RICHARDS, Sir Gordon b. 1905. English champion jockey. The first jockey to be knighted.

RICHELIEU, Armand Jean du Plessis, Duc de 1585–1642. Cardinal Richelieu. Virtual ruler of France as Chief Minister under **Louis XIII**. One of the most important French historical figures.
An autograph as cardinal and a more careful signature. Also signature as Bishop of Luçon.

RICHTER, Hans 1843–1916. Hungarian composer. Authority on the music of his friend and associate **Wagner**.

RICHTHOFEN, Manfred, Baron von 1882–1918. German airman. The most famous of the World War I 'aces'. He shot down 80 Allied planes before he was himself killed in action.

RIEBEECK, Jan (Johan) Van 1618–77. Dutch colonial administrator. The founder of the colonisation of South Africa and of Capetown.
His signature with that of another member of his Committee to a Resolution, Cape of Good Hope, 1652. (Cape Archives.)

R

RILKE, Rainer Maria 1875–1926. German
lyric and philosophic poet.
A poetical holograph and an unconnected
signature.

RIMBAUD (J) (N) Arthur 1854–91.
Belgian-born French symbolist poet.

RIMSKY-KORSAKOV, Nikolai An-
dreievich 1844–1908. Russian composer of
operas such as *The Snow Maiden*, the
symphonic poem *Scheherazade* and other
works, including *Flight of the Bumblebee*.

RIVERA, Diego 1886–1957. Mexican
painter of murals, etc.
His holograph on his visiting card.

DIEGO RIVERA

ALTA VISTA Y LAS PALMAS
VILLA OBREGON, D. F.

TELEFONOS
5·90·55 — 5·91·21

ROBERTS (OF KANDAHAR), Frederick
S, Earl 1832–1914. British soldier. C-in-C in
South African War 1899–1900.

ROBESON, Paul 1898–1976. American
Negro singer and actor. Took leading roles
in several films and on the stage where he
was a success as Othello in particular.

ROBESPIERRE, Maximilian F M I de 1758–94. The outstanding personality of the French Revolution. Leader of the Jacobins. Responsible for the 'Reign of Terror', he himself perished by the guillotine.

Also DS by the Committee of Public Safety, signed by four members of this all-powerful Committee, Robespierre, **Carnot**, Collot-d'Herbois and Barère, decreeing that a Corporal Le Mot, being a sculptor, be released from military duties to portray the glories of the Revolution. An added interest is that the document is in the holograph of **Jacques Louis David**, the greatest of the Napoleonic portrait and historical painters. He was Secretary of the Committee. Dated Paris 11 floréal an 11 (30 April 1794). (Author's Collection.)

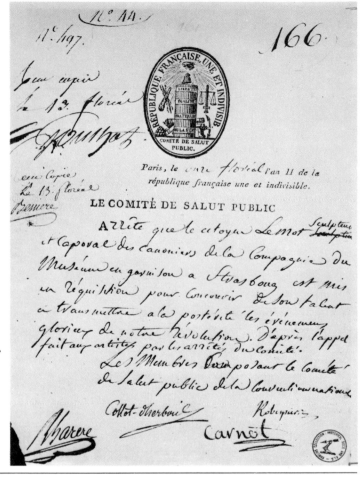

ROBEY, Sir George 1869–1954. English comedian. 'The Prime Minister of Mirth'. Signed self-caricature. (Author's Collection.) Robey frequently caricatured himself and this example, the original of which is in blue and red ink, is typical.

ROBINSON 'Sugar' Ray b. 1920. American boxer. Originally Walker Smith, jnr. Five times (a world record) World Middleweight Champion.

R

ROBINSON, William Heath 1872–1944. British humorous artist. Brought a new word to the language by his 'Heath Robinson' drawings of ridiculously complicated devices for performing elementary actions.

ROCHAMBEAU, (J) (B) Donatien de Vimeur, Comte de 1725–1807. French soldier. Greatly assisted **Washington** in the American War of Independence.

ROCHEFOUCAULD, François, Duc de La 1613–80. French writer. Author of the *Maximes*.

ROCKEFELLER, John D(avison) 1839–1937. American oil magnate and philanthropist.

ROCKINGHAM, Charles Watson-Wentworth, Marquis of 1730–82. English statesman. Twice Prime Minister.
See also with British Prime Ministers page 68.

RODGERS, Richard (Charles) b. 1902. American composer. Wrote the scores for the musicals *The King and I* and *The Sound of Music*.

RODIN, (F) Auguste (R) 1840–1917. French sculptor of such masterpieces as *The Kiss*, *The Thinker* and the statue of **Balzac**.

RODNEY, George B, Lord 1719–1792. British Admiral. Won the significant victory of the battle off Domenica against the French 1782.

ROGERS, Will. In full William Penn Adair 1879–1935. American actor and humorist. Starred in many film comedies and wrote such works as *Letters of a Self-Made Diplomat to his President*.

ROLFE, Frederick 'Baron Corvo' 1860–1913. English writer. Known for his novel *Hadrian the Seventh*.
A J A Symons wrote the biography of this witty, learned eccentric, *The Quest for Corvo*. Scarce signature and portion of holograph manuscript from his commonplace book of 1901. (Donald Weeks Collection.)

ROLLAND, Romain 1866–1944. French author. Won Nobel Prize, 1915. Biographer of **Handel**, **Tolstoy** and **Gandhi**.

ROMMEL, Erwin 1891–1944. The most brilliant of the German Army commanders in World War II. Field Marshal Rommel, 'the Desert Fox', died by his own hand after implication in a plot to kill **Hitler**.

ROMNEY, George 1734–1802. English painter. Executed many portraits of Lady **Hamilton**.

RONSARD, Pierre de 1524–85. French lyric poet. Leader of the Pléiade.
A very rare signature.

RÖNTGEN, Wilhelm K 1845–1923. German Nobel Prize-winning physicist. The discoverer of X-rays.
A typical example of his tiny autograph.

ROOSEVELT, Franklin Delano 1882–1945. Thirty-second President of the USA 1933–45. Leader of his country in World War II. Initiated the 'New Deal'.
See also with US Presidents page 205.

ROOSEVELT, Theodore 1858–1919. Twenty-sixth President of the USA. Won the Nobel Peace Prize, 1906 as mediator in the Russo-Japanese War.
See also with US Presidents page 205.

R

ROSA, Salvator 1615–73. Italian painter and poet.

ROSAS, Juan Manuel de 1793–1877. Argentinian soldier-politician. Dictator 1835–52.

ROSEBERY, Archibald P Primrose, 5th Earl of 1847–1929. British Prime Minister. See also with British Prime Ministers page 69.

ROSS, Sir John 1777–1856. Scottish Arctic explorer. Attempted the Northwest Passage and searched for Sir **John Franklin**.

ROSS, Sir Ronald 1857–1932. British physician who discovered the malaria parasite. Won Nobel Prize for Medicine, 1902.

ROSSETTI, Christina G 1830–94. British poetess.

ROSSETTI, Dante Gabriel 1828–82. British poet and painter aligned with the Pre-Raphaelites.

ROSSINI, Gioacchino A 1792–1868. Italian composer of the operas *William Tell*, *The Barber of Seville*, amongst others.

ROSTAND, Edmond 1868–1918. French dramatist and poet. Wrote the play in verse *Cyrano de Bergerac*.

ROTHSCHILD, Mayer (or Meyer) Amschel 1743–1812. German Jewish founder of the banking house of Rothschild.
This autograph and that of **Nathan Rothschild** below are from the collection of Mr Julius Bisno of Los Angeles, USA.

ROTHSCHILD, Baron Nathan Mayer (or Meyer) 1777–1836. Son of **Mayer Amschel Rothschild**, he founded the London branch of the family banking business.

ROUGET de LISLE, Claude Joseph 1760–1836. French Revolutionary soldier and writer who composed the 'Marseillaise'.

ROUND (LITTLE), Dorothy b. 1909. British lawn tennis player. Won Wimbledon Ladies Singles in 1934 and 1937 and many other championships.

ROUSSEAU, Jean Jacques 1712–78. French philosopher and writer. Signature and holograph MSS notes. (Author's Collection.)

RUBENS, Peter Paul 1577–1640. Flemish master painter.
A highly important art autograph.

RUBINSTEIN, Anton 1829–94. Russian composer and pianist.

R

RUBINSTEIN, Artur b. 1888. Polish-born American pianist.

RUPERT, Count Palatine of the Rhine 1619–82. Prince 'Rupert of the Rhine', 'The Mad Cavalier'. Dashing cavalry leader under **Charles I**. A founder of the Hudson's Bay Company and a scientist.

RUSKIN, John 1819–1900. English art critic and man of letters.
An unusual ALS discussing the possible production of a cheap edition of his *The Queen of the Air*, provided his correspondent can get 'a hundred signatures of real workmen, in Blackburn or elsewhere, asking for it'. (Author's Collection.)

RUSSELL, John, 1st Earl (Lord John Russell) 1792–1878. British Liberal statesman.
See also with British Prime Ministers page 69.

RUSSELL, Bertrand (A) (W), 3rd Earl 1872–1970. British philosopher and mathematician. Won Nobel Literature Prize, 1950.

RUTH, George Herman, 'Babe Ruth' 1895–1948. The greatest name in baseball. Scored a record 714 home runs in his career in the American major league.

RUTHERFORD, Ernest Lord 1871–1937. British physicist. Distinguished for his work on the structure of the atom. Won Nobel Chemistry Prize, 1908.

RUYTER, Michiel A de 1607–76. Dutch naval hero. A frequent adversary of **Blake** and **Monck**. Admiral-in-Chief of his country's navy.

SADAT, Anwar b. 1918. Egyptian statesman. Succeeded **G A Nasser** as President of his country.

SADE, Donatien A F, Marquis de 1740–1814. French author of obscene and cruel novels revealing the perversion named after him 'sadism'. Also see with Dictionary Names page 110.

SAINT-SAËNS, (C) Camille 1835–1921. French composer. Commenced composing at the age of 16. He was also a pianist, organist and conductor.

ST VINCENT, John Jervis, Earl of 1735–1823. British Admiral who defeated the Spanish Fleet off Cape St Vincent, 1797.

SALISBURY, Robert A T G Cecil, 3rd Marquess of 1830–1903. English statesman. Three times Premier.
See also with British Prime Ministers page 69.

SALOTE (TUPOU), 1900–65. Queen of Tonga 1918–65.

SAND, George, pseudonym of A Aurore Dudevant (*née* Dupin) 1804–76. French writer who formed liaisons with **A de Musset**, **Chopin** and others.
An ALS to a male friend signed 'ton lézard vert' (your green lizard). (Author's Collection.) Also her usual signature.

SANDWICH, John Montagu, 4th Earl of 1718–92. English politician. Invented the 'sandwich' to eat at the gaming table.
See also with Dictionary Names page 110.

SAN MARTÍN, José de 1778–1850. South American patriot and soldier. Born in the Argentine. Led liberation forces against the Spanish. Established the independence of Chile and of Peru.

SANSON, Charles Henri 1740–95. Public executioner of the French Revolution. Executed **Louis XVI**.

SANTA ANNA, Antonio López de *c.* 1796–1876. Mexican nationalist leader and patriot. Four times President.

SARASATE, 'Pablo' (Martin M) de 1844–1908. Spanish violinist and composer.

SARGENT, John Singer 1856–1925. American painter who worked mostly in Britain.

SARTRE, Jean-Paul b. 1905. French existentialist philosopher, dramatist and novelist.
An example of his holograph.

SASSOON, Siegfried (L) 1886–1967. English poet and novelist. *Memoirs of a Fox-Hunting Man* won him the Hawthornden Prize in 1929.

SAVANG VATTHANA, Sri b. 1907. King of Laos, 1959–74.

SAVONAROLA, Girolamo 1452–98. Italian Dominican monk and reformer who rose to rule Florence but, losing power, was tortured, hanged and burned to death.

SAXE, Maurice, Comte de 1696–1750. Marshal Saxe. A bastard prince of Saxony, he served brilliantly in the French Army.

SAYERS, Dorothy L 1893–1957. English detective-novel writer. Creator of 'Lord Peter Wimsey'.

SCARLATTI, Alessandro 1659–1725. Italian composer.
Autographically very rare.

SCHEELE, Carl Wilhelm 1742–86. Swedish chemist. Discoverer of chlorine, nitrogen and manganese. Isolated glycerin.
A scarce autograph.

SCHILLER, J C Friedrich von 1759–1805. Other than **Goethe**, the major name in German literature. A master poet and historical dramatist.
Variant autographs in German and italic styles.

SCHMIDT, Helmut H W b. 1918. German statesman. Chancellor of the Federal Republic of (West) Germany, 1974.

SCHOPENHAUER, Arthur 1788–1860. German pessimist philosopher.

SCHREINER, Olive 1855–1920. South African authoress of the classic *The Story of an African Farm.*

SCHUBERT, Franz (Peter) 1797–1828. Austrian composer particularly famed for his songs. A scarce and important musical autograph. Signature and holograph music. (British Library.)

SCHUMANN, Robert (A) 1810–56. German composer.
A scarce musical autograph. A signed holograph receipt for £50.00 for his Opus 85. (Author's Collection.)

SCHWEITZER, Albert 1875–1965. Alsatian-French medical missionary, theologian, philosopher, musician and man of peace. Schweitzer used an amaneunsis to write most of his letters in a hand and with a signature very similar to his own. Experts are not all in agreement over certain identification of Schweitzer autographs. The top autograph shown here is definitely genuine and reproduced by kind permission of Mr Charles Hamilton, the New York expert.

SCOTT, Robert Falcon 1868–1912. 'Scott of the Antarctic'. British explorer who reached the South Pole, but perished on the return journey.

SCOTT, Sir Walter 1771–1832. Scottish novelist and poet. Author of *Waverley*, *Marmion*, *Ivanhoe* and *The Lay of the Last Minstrel*. Scott has been the subject of many autographic forgeries but the most confusing 'Scott' item is a very realistic facsimile of a half-page letter to Charles Tilt, referring to himself as the author of *Waverley* of which many copies are still being offered for sale.

SCRIBE, A Eugène 1791–1861. French dramatist. He was also the librettist of several operas, including **Auber**'s *Fra Diavolo* and **Meyerbeer**'s *Robert le Diable*.

SEABORG, Glenn Theodore b. 1912. American chemist. Co-discoverer of the elements plutonium, americium, curium, berkelium, californium, mendelevium and element 102. Won Nobel Chemistry Prize, 1951.

SÉRURIER, Jaume M P, Comte de 1742–1819. French Marshal of the Empire. See also with Napoleonic Marshals page 179.

SHACKLETON, Sir Ernest (Henry) 1874–1922. British Antarctic explorer.

The Presidents of the United States of America

There have been 39 Presidents of whom one, Grover Cleveland, was both the 22nd and 24th. The most sought-after autographically are Lincoln and Washington.

Autograph material of the Presidents is, as a general rule, more scarce when written during their periods of office than at other times in their careers. This applies in particular to Presidents Garfield, Taylor, Arthur, Andrew Johnson and McKinley. W H Harrison is even more rare of Presidential date as he died only one month after taking over as President.

President Lincoln is the most forged, whilst all Presidents from Harding onwards permitted their secretaries to sign for them in the same style as their own signatures. President Hoover was the worst offender as regards facsimile notes and President Truman also resorted to these. The autopen has also added to the confusion in more recent years and President Kennedy, in particular, not only permitted its use but allowed several of his secretaries to reproduce his signature to the extent that his is now the most difficult of all the Presidential autographs to authenticate. President Nixon's signature has varied considerably and there is a more typical example at page 167.

Many useful evaluations and discussions of Presidential autographs have been published. Of these the chapter on the Presidents in Charles Hamilton's valuable work *Collecting Autographs and Manuscripts* (Norman, 1961), and Mary Benjamin's outstanding booklet *The Presidents* (Benjamin, 1965), which take one up to Presidents Kennedy and L B Johnson respectively, are two of the most helpful.

The signatures of all the Presidents are shown here in historical order with their dates of holding office. All are from the group of Presidential facsimile signatures kindly provided by the Library of Congress, Washington DC, except for the second example of Grover Cleveland. In the case of

20

21

22

23

24

25

26

27

28

29

30

31

32

33

34

35

36

37

Sincerely,

Richard Nixon

38

39

Jimmy Carter

this President another specimen of his autograph has been used to make for more interesting comparison. This has been taken from the Author's Collection, also President Carter from Mrs. J. Enders. Presidential dates are shown below.

1. George Washington. 1789–97.
2. John Adams. 1797–1801.
3. Thomas Jefferson. 1801–9.
4. James Madison. 1809–17.
5. James Monroe. 1817–25.
6. John Quincy Adams. 1825–9.
7. Andrew Jackson. 1829–37.
8. Martin Van Buren. 1837–41.
9. William H Harrison. 4 March–4 April 1841.
10. John Tyler. 1841–5.
11. James K Polk. 1845–9.
12. Zachary Taylor. 1849–50.
13. Millard Fillmore. 1850–3.
14. Franklin Pierce. 1853–7.
15. James Buchanan. 1857–61.
16. Abraham Lincoln. 1861–5.
17. Andrew Johnson. 1865–9.
18. Ulysses S Grant. 1869–77.
19. Rutherford B Hayes. 1877–81.
20. James A Garfield. 4 March–19 September 1881
21. Chester A Arthur. 1881–5.
22. Grover Cleveland. 1885–9.
23. Benjamin Harrison. 1889–93.
24. Grover Cleveland. 1893–7.
25. William McKinley. 1897–1901.
26. Theodore Roosevelt. 1901–9.
27. William H Taft. 1909–13.
28. Woodrow Wilson. 1913–21.
29. Warren G Harding. 1921–3.
30. Calvin Coolidge. 1923–9.
31. Herbert C Hoover. 1929–33.
32. Franklin D Roosevelt. 1933–45.
33. Harry S Truman. 1945–53.
34. Dwight D Eisenhower. 1953–61.
35. John F Kennedy. 1961–3.
36. Lyndon B Johnson. 1963–9.
37. Richard M Nixon. 1969–74.
38. Gerald R Ford. 1974–77.
39. Jimmy Carter. 1977–.

S

SHAKESPEARE, William 1564–1616. English dramatist and poet. The most famous name in English literature. Autographically, it must be said, Shakespeare is very unsatisfactory! Here shown are the only six extant signatures fully accepted as genuine. Shakespeare's autograph has been frequently forged, in particular by William Ireland (1777–1835).

The signatures shown are to be found as follows:

1. On a conveyance for a house in Blackfriars, London, 1613. (The Guildhall, City of London Library.)
2. On a deposition in the Belott-Mountjoy suit, 1612. (The Public Record Office, London.)
3, 4 and 5. On the three pages of Shakespeare's will. (British (Museum) Library.)
6. On a mortgage, 1613. (British (Museum) Library.)

Each of these signatures, even the three written at the same time as each other on his Will, differs from the others. The spelling even differs in some cases. All six are in the old secretary hand and are cramped and awkward whereas his contemporaries, **Bacon** and **Jonson**, were beginning to employ the flowing italic script. The fact that only signatures definitely exist and that nothing autograph of Shakespeare's own prolific works has remained in existence, adds to the arguments concerning the authorship of his plays. This controversy is, however, not for autographers. We can only express our mystification at the glaring differences in style and spelling of the surviving signatures.

A portion of *The Book of Sir Thomas More* shown here is regarded by a number of experts as being in his hand. This work is largely in the holograph of Anthony Munday a little-known contemporary of Shakespeare, but was revised and added to by at least four other writers as five differing hands are discernible.

It is thought that one of these may well have been that of Shakespeare and that certain pages could be entirely in his autograph. The matter is discussed by the distinguished authority on autographs, P J Croft, Librarian of King's College, Cambridge in his work *Autograph Poetry of the English Language* (2 vols. Cassell, 1973), page 9.

SHAW, George Bernard 1856–1950. British dramatist and critic. His many works include *Man and Superman*, *Saint Joan* and *Pygmalion*. The last-named was adapted as the musical play *My Fair Lady*. Won Nobel Prize, 1925.
The end of an ALS with a typical Shavian comment. (Author's Collection.)

SHELBURNE, William Petty, Marquess of Lansdowne and 2nd Earl of 1737–1805. English statesman.
See also with British Prime Ministers page 68.

SHELLEY, Mary Wollstonecraft 1797–1851. Shelley's second wife. Author of *Frankenstein* and thus the somewhat surprising creator of the 'Monster' who still survives in 'horror' films today.

SHELLEY, Percy Bysshe 1792–1822. English poet.
His early death adds to the rarity of Shelley's autograph.

SHERIDAN, Richard Brinsley 1751–1816. British dramatist known for *The School for Scandal* and *The Rivals*.

SHOSTAKOVICH, Dmitri D 1906–75. Russian composer, particularly known for his symphonies.
Signed autograph music. (Author's Collection.)

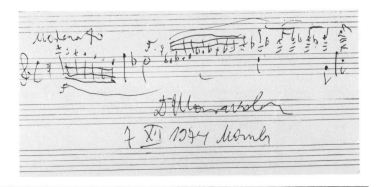

SIBELIUS, Jean 1865–1957. the doyen of Finnish composers. Famed for his symphonic poem *Finlandia*.
Sibelius frequently signed in pencil as in this example.

SIDDONS, Sarah 1755–1831. English actress. A great tragedienne. Associated with **Garrick** she was probably the most distinguished actress in the history of British theatre.

SIDMOUTH, Henry Addington, Viscount 1757–1844. English statesman.
See also with British Prime Ministers page 68.

SIDNEY, Sir Philip 1554–86. English poet who died a soldier's death after the battle of Zutphen.

SIEMENS, E Werner von 1816–92. German engineer. Constructed Germany's first telegraph line. Invented a self-acting dynamo. Discovered the insulating properties of gutta-percha.

SIENKIEWICZ, Henrik 1846–1916. Polish Nobel Prize-winning (1905) novelist who wrote *Quo Vadis?*.

SIHANOUK, Prince Norodom b. 1922. Cambodian statesman. King 1941–45, Abdicated and remained Prime Minister. Exiled to China. Supported the capture of his country by the Communists.

SIKORSKY, Igor I b. 1889. Russian-born, American aeronautical engineer. Built the first four-engine plane and invented the first successful helicopter.

SILHOUETTE, Étienne de 1709–1767. French Finance Minister whose unpopular reforms led to his name being given, as a shadow, to the outline drawing 'silhouette'. See also with Dictionary Names page 110.

SIMENON, Georges, pen name of Georges Sim, b 1903. Belgian novelist. Creator of the detective 'Maigret'.

SIMPSON, Sir James Young 1811–70. Scottish physician. Pioneer of anaesthetics.

SINATRA, 'Frank' (Francis Albert) b. 1915. American singer and film actor.

SISLEY, Alfred 1839–99. French impressionist landscape painter of English descent.

SITTING BULL, 1834–90. Sioux Indian chief and leader in the Sioux War 1876–7. Ambushed and wiped out **Custer** and all his men at the Little Big Horn.
Variant examples of his rare signature.

SITWELL, Dame Edith 1887–1964. English poetess. Sister of Sir **Osbert** and Sir **Sacheverell Sitwell**.

SITWELL, Sir Osbert 1892–1969. English author, brother of **Edith Sitwell**. His five-volume autobiography, (the first volume was *Left Hand: Right Hand* and the last *Noble Essences*) was completed in 1950.

SITWELL, Sir Sacheverell b. 1897. Poet and art critic. Brother of **Edith** and Sir **Osbert Sitwell**.

SLOCUM, Joshua 1844–1910. American mariner. The first man to sail alone round the world, 1895–8. An example of his autograph written at Cape Town, 12 January 1898 whilst on his world voyage on his yacht *Spray*. (Author's Collection.)

SMETANA, Bedřich 1824–84. Czech composer.
Variant examples of his uncommon autograph.

SMITH, Sir C Aubrey 1863–1948. British film actor and cricketer.
See also pig drawn blindfold page 147.

SMOLLETT, Tobias G 1721–71. Scots novelist.
Uncommon autographically.

SMUTS, Jan Christiaan 1870–1950. South African statesman. Twice Prime Minister. A Boer General in the South African War. A member of the War Cabinet in both world wars and a British Field Marshal.

SMYTH, Pat(ricia) (Koechlin) b. 1928. British Olympic horsewoman. She won three successive European show-jumping titles 1961–3.

SNELL, Peter (George) b. 1938. New Zealand Olympic champion at 800 metres in 1960 and at both 800 and 1500 metres in 1964.

SOBHUZA II, b. 1899. King Ngwenyama)
of Swaziland. The world's longest reigning
monarch, since December 1899.

SOLZHENITSYN, Alexander b. 1918.
Russian novelist. Won Nobel Literature
Prize, 1970.

SOMERSET, Edward Seymour, Duke of *c.*
1506–52. Protector of the Realm of England
during the minority of **Edward VI**.

SOULT, Nicolas Jean de Dieu, Duke of
Dalmatia 1769–1851. French Marshal under **Napoleon** and Minister of War under
the restored Bourbons. See also with Napoleonic Marshals page 179.

SOUSA, John Philip 1854–1932. American
composer. 'The March King'. Famed for
such marches as 'The Washington Post' and
'Stars and Stripes Forever'. He also wrote
comic operas. Signature and PS with
musical bars. (Author's Collection.)

SOUTHEY, Robert 1774–1843. One of the
English Lake poets, he became Poet Laureate.

SOYER, Alexis 1809–58. The most celebrated cook of the 19th century. A French-
man, he was chef at the Reform Club in
London, also adviser during the Irish famine
of 1847 and on the food system in the
Crimea, 1855.

SPEED, John 1542–1629. English cartographer and antiquary. Executed 54 *Maps of
England and Wales*.

SPEKE, John Hanning 1827–64. English explorer in Africa. Discovered Victoria, Nyanza.

SPENCE, Sir Basil U 1907–76. British architect. Designed Coventry Cathedral. Also responsible for the controversial Household Cavalry Barracks at Knightsbridge.

SPENDER, Stephen b. 1909. British poet and critic. Also noted for his translations of **Rilke**, **Schiller**, **Toller** and **Garcia Lorca**.

SPENSER, Edmund *c.* 1552–99. English Elizabethan poet. His most successful work was *The Faerie Queene*.

SPINOZA, Baruch de 1632–77. Dutch-Jewish philosopher.
An important and scarce autograph. Variant examples, the two using a small 's' the other a capital 'S'.

SPITZ, Mark (Andrew) b. 1950. American swimmer. One of the greatest of all time, he won, uniquely, seven gold medals in a single Olympic Games, 1972.

SPOCK, Benjamin M b. 1903. American paediatrician whose book *The Common-Sense Book of Baby and Child Care* was a world record commercially best-selling non-fiction work.

SPOONER, William A 1844–1930. English clergyman and educationalist whose transposition of letters and word sounds led to 'spoonerisms' named after him; for example, 'a blushing crow' for 'a crushing blow' and 'a half-warmed fish' for 'a half-formed wish'. See also with Dictionary Names page 110.

SPURZHEIM, Johann C C 1776–1832. German physician. Co-founder of phrenology.

'SPY', pen name of Sir Leslie Ward 1851–1922. English caricaturist. Signed sketch of pigs. (Author's Collection.) Also see 'pig' drawn blindfold page 147.

STAËL, (A) (L) Germaine, Madame de 1766–1817. French woman of letters and intellectual leader. Daughter of **Necker**. Signature as Baroness de Staël-Holstein.

STAFFORD, Thomas P b. 1930. American astronaut. The first man to rendezvous in space, 1965. Commanded Apollo craft on dramatic link-up in space with Soviet Soyuz, 1975. See PS with Leonov at page 136.

STALIN, Joseph. Correctly Josif Vissarionovich Dzhugashvili 1879–1953. Soviet statesman. Took a prominent part in the 1917 Revolution and subsequently became all-powerful as General Secretary of the Communist Party, 1922. Virtual dictator from 1926. Was also Prime Minister from 1941 and guided Russia's fortunes throughout World War II and thereafter until his death.

His rare signature shown here on a card signed with others at the time of the Potsdam Conference, 1945. The signatories are, from top to bottom, 1. **Clement Attlee**; 2. **Ernest Bevin**; 3. **Andrei Vyshinsky** with autograph date and place – Potsdam; 4. **Joseph Stalin**; 5. **V M Molotov**. (Author's Collection.)

STANLEY, Sir Henry Morton 1841–1904. British explorer who found **Livingstone** at Ujiji and, after other African explorations, founded the Congo State.

STEELE, Sir Richard 1672–1729. English writer. Founded, with **Addison**, *The Tatler* and *The Spectator* and managed Drury Lane Theatre.

STEINBECK, John (E) 1902–68. American novelist. Wrote *The Grapes of Wrath*, *Of Mice and Men*, etc. Won Nobel Prize, 1962.

STENDHAL, pseudonym of Marie Henri Beyle 1783–1842. French writer. Variant signatures as 'Beyle' and as 'F Brenier', another pseudonym, rare autographically.

STEPHENSON, George 1781–1848. English inventor. The founder of railways. Constructed the famous 'Rocket' locomotive.
A sought-after autograph.

STERNE, Laurence 1713–68. English author of sentimental, witty novels, notably *The Life and Opinions of Tristram Shandy* and *A Sentimental Journey through France and Italy*.

STEVENSON, Robert Louis 1850–94. Scottish author of *Treasure Island*, *Kidnapped*, *The Black Arrow* and *The Master of Ballantrae*. A scarce and important British literary autograph. Shown here is a delightful little ALS in which he gently points out to a Londoner that Samoa is no further away from him than London is from his correspondent! Dated at Vailima, 7 December 1893. Stevenson died less than a year later. (Author's Collection.)

STEWART, 'Jackie'. John Young Stewart b. 1939. Scots racing motorist. World Champion driver in 1969, 1971 and 1973. He won a record 27 Grand Prix. PS. (Author's Collection.)

STILL, William Grant b. 1895. American Negro composer. Known for his *Afro American Symphony*.

STOKER, Bram, correctly Abraham 1847–1912. Irish-born writer of *Dracula*, etc. See also autographic remarks under **Irving**. His signature was often even less regular than this example.

STOWE, Harriet Beecher 1811–96. American abolitionist novelist famed for *Uncle Tom's Cabin*.

STRADIVARI(US), Antonio *c*. 1644–1737. Italian violin-maker of Cremona. A valuable and rare autograph.

STRAFFORD, Thomas Wentworth, Earl of 1593–1641. Chief adviser and favourite of **Charles I**. Impeached and executed by Parliament.

STRAUSS, Johann, the Elder 1804–49. Austrian conductor and composer of over 150 waltzes. 'The Father of the Waltz'.

S

STRAUSS, Johann, the Younger 1825–99. 'The Waltz King'. Viennese composer and conductor. Wrote the operetta *Die Fledermaus* and the waltz *The Blue Danube*.
Though more in demand, his autograph is less scarce than that of his father. Also a differing signature. PS. (Author's Collection.)

STRAUSS, Richard (G) 1864–1949. German composer of the operas *Der Rosenkavalier* and *Salome*.

STRAVINSKY, Igor 1882–1971. Russian composer.
Autograph music from *Rite of Spring*. (Author's Collection.)

STRINDBERG, (J) August 1849–1912. Swedish dramatist and novelist. His work includes *Fröken Julie* and *Fadren*.

STUART, Prince Charles Edward 1720–88. 'The Young Pretender' or 'Bonnie Prince Charlie'. Grandson of **James II**. Attempted to regain his grandfather's throne. Signs 'Charles R'(ex) as 'King'.

STUART, Prince James Edward 1688–1766. 'The Old Pretender', 'James III'. Son of **James II**, he struggled to regain his father's throne. Signature, in French as if King – 'Jacques R(ex)'.

STUYVESANT, Peter 1592–1672. Dutch colonial administrator. Regarded as the founder of New York, then New Amsterdam.
Part of an autograph marginal note on a petition. (Library of Congress, USA.)

SUCHET, Louis Gabriel, Duc d'Albufera 1772–1826. French Marshal.
See also with Napoleonic Marshals page 179.

SULLIVAN, Sir Arthur S 1842–1900. British composer particularly of operettas in conjunction with the librettist, Sir **W S Gilbert**.
Autograph musical extract from *Trial by Jury*. (Author's Collection.)

SULLY, Maximilien de Béthune, Duc de 1560–1641. French statesman and soldier. Finance Minister of **Henry IV**.
Variant signatures.

SUN YAT-SEN, 1866–1925. Chinese revolutionary patriot and nationalist leader. First President of the Chinese Republic, 1912.

S-T

SUSANN, Jacqueline (Mrs Irving Mansfield) 1921–74. American writer. Sales of her *Valley of the Dolls* reached 15,800,000 copies in June 1973, creating a world record for novels.

SUTHERLAND, Graham V b. 1903. English painter. Executed portraits of **Churchill** and **Maugham** and the tapestry *Christ in Majesty* in Coventry Cathedral.

SUTHERLAND, Joan b. 1926. Australian prima donna.

SWEDENBORG, Emanuel 1688–1772. Swedish mystic, metaphysicist and religious philosopher. His followers, the Swedenborgians, are still established as the New Jerusalem Church.

SWIFT, Jonathan 1667–1745. English satirist. Dean of St Patrick's, Dublin. Author of *Gulliver's Travels*.
Variant autographs.

SWINBURNE, Algernon Charles 1837–1909. English poet.

SYNGE, J(ohn) M(illington) 1871–1909. Irish playwright. His masterpiece is perhaps the comedy *The Playboy of the Western World*. An early example of his signature on a French student card. A scarce autograph.

TAFT, William Howard 1857–1930. Twenty-seventh President of the USA. See signature with US Presidents page 205.

TAGORE, Sir Rabindranath 1861–1941. Indian poet and philosopher. The first Asian to win a Nobel Prize for Literature, 1913.

TALBOT, W Henry Fox 1800–77. English pioneer of photography. Produced the first book, *Pencil of Nature*, ever to be illustrated photographically.

TALLEYRAND (-PÉRIGORD), Charles Maurice, Prince de Benevento 1754–1838. French statesman under **Napoleon** and the Bourbons. An important but not yet scarce French political autograph.

TALLIEN, Jean Lambert 1769–1820. French Revolutionary. Became President of the Convention and overthrew **Robespierre**.

TALMA, François Joseph 1763 1826. French tragedian and stage-costume reformer.

TASMAN, Abel J 1603–59. Dutch navigator who discovered New Zealand, Tonga and Van Diemen's Land, now Tasmania.

TASSO, Torquato 1544–95. Italian poet. Wrote the epic poem *Jerusalem Delivered* and the pastoral play *Aminta*.
Widely variant signatures, the one using only his Christian name and paraph.

TAYLOR, Elizabeth b. 1932. Anglo-American film actress. Twice married to actor Richard Burton.

TAYLOR, Zachary 1784–1850. Twelfth President of the USA. A successful General in the War with Mexico.
See also with US Presidents page 204.

T

TEMPLE, Shirley b. 1928. American child film actress, singer and dancer. Now Mrs Charles Black, she has been US Ambassador to Ghana.

TENNIEL, Sir John 1820–1914. English political cartoonist and illustrator of *Alice in Wonderland*, etc.

TENNYSON, Alfred, Lord 1809–92. British Poet Laureate. The first poet to be created a peer for his poetic work. **Macaulay** (and others) were ennobled for other services.

TENZING NORKAY, b. 1914. Nepalese mountaineer. With **Hillary** first to climb Mount Everest, 1953.

TERESA (OF AVILA), Saint 1515–82. Spanish Saint and mystic who founded a reformed order of Carmelite nuns. Canonised 1622.

TERESA (OF CALCUTTA), Mother. Roman Catholic missionary in India. She has spent a lifetime of work for the poor.

TERESHKOVA (-NIKOLAYEV), Valentina V b. 1937. Soviet cosmonaut. The first woman in space, June 1963.

TERRY, Dame Ellen (A) 1848–1928. English actress. Established a formidable acting partnership with **Sir Henry Irving**.

TETRAZZINI, Luisa 1871–1940. Italian coloratura soprano singer.

THACKERAY, William Makepeace 1811–63. English novelist. In addition to using two styles of writing (see examples), Thackeray occasionally signed pseudonyms such as 'Titmarsh', 'Yellowplush', 'Fitzboodle' and 'Wagstaff'!
An example of his sloping hand and of his more often used upright hand.

THATCHER, Margaret (Hilda) b. 1925. English politician. The first woman to lead a British political party, the Conservatives, 1975.
PS. (Author's Collection.)

THIERS, Louis Adolphe 1797–1877. French statesman and historian. President 1871–3.

THIEU, Nguyen van. President of South Vietnam 1965–75.

THOMAS AQUINAS, Saint 1225–74. Italian Scholastic philosopher and theologian. A Dominican, he established Thomism. His greatest written work was *Summa Theologica*. A specimen of his holograph.

THOMAS, Dylan (M) 1914–53. Welsh poet.
Though modern, his autograph is uncommon and sought after.

THOMSON, Sir Joseph John 1856–1940. Nobel Prize-winning British nuclear physicist who discovered the isotope and made important observations in the study of the electron.

221

T

THOREAU, Henry David 1817–62. American writer.

THORNDIKE, Dame Sybil 1882–1976. English actress.

'THUMB, General Tom' stage name of Charles S Stratton *c.* 1832–83. American midget. Only 30½ in tall at 18, he continued to grow as an adult to 35 in at 30 and 40 in at his death.

TIEPOLO, Giovanni Battista 1696–1770. The last of the great Venetian painters. An example of his painting signature.

TILDEN, William T 1893–1953. 'Big Bill', American tennis player. Three times Wimbledon and seven times American Singles Champion.

TINTORETTO, Real name Giacomo or Jacopo Robusti 1518–94. One of the greatest of the Venetian painters. His painting style signature.

TIPPETT, Sir Michael b. 1905. British composer. Signed autograph musical extract. (By kind permission of Sir Michael Tippett.)

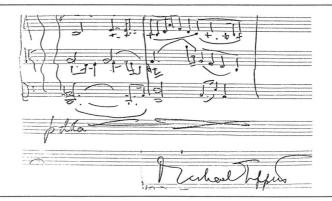

TIRPITZ, Alfred P F von 1849–1930. German Admiral. Secretary of State for the Imperial Navy 1897–1916, he was also Commander-in-Chief of the German Navy 1914–16.

TITIAN, correctly Tiziano Vecelli(o) ?–1576. Italian painter. The great master of the Venetian school.
An example of the many different signatures used on his paintings.

Tizianus · F ·

TITO, Josip Broz, Marshal b. 1892. Yugoslav soldier, patriot and statesman. Premier 1945–53. President thereafter.

TITOV, Gherman Stepanovich b. 1935. Soviet cosmonaut, the second Russian in space, August 1961.

TOGO, Marquis Heihachiro 1847–1934. Japanese Admiral. As C-in-C Japanese Fleet, he destroyed the enemy fleets in the Russo-Japanese War.
Signature as Count.

TOLLER, Ernst 1893–1939. German dramatist, poet and political reformer.

TOLSTOY, Count Leo N 1828–1910. Russian novelist, social philosopher and mystic. His great works include *War and Peace* and *Anna Karenina*.

TOSCANINI, Arturo 1867–1957. Italian conductor, possibly the greatest of his age. Toscanini frequently used red ink. The original of this example is in that colour.

TOSTI, Sir (F) Paolo 1846–1916. Italian-born British naturalised composer, particularly of songs such as his 'Goodbye'.

TOULOUSE-LAUTREC, Henri M R de 1864–1901. French painter, known for his portrayal of Parisian life and characters in poster designs and lithographs.
A fairly scarce and sought-after autograph.

TOUSSAINT-L'OUVERTURE, Pierre Dominique 1743–1803. Haitian Negro patriot and revolutionary. Born a slave, he rose to be the Island's administrator.

TREVITHICK, Richard 1771–1833. English engineer and inventor. Built first steam locomotive to run on rails. Trevithick's signature is sometimes less elaborate than this example.

TROLLOPE, Anthony 1815–82. English novelist. Known in particular for his *Barchester* series.

TROMP, Cornelis van 1629–91. Dutch Admiral. Son of **Maarten van Tromp**. Fought many engagements against the combined English and French fleets.

TROMP, Maarten Harpertszoon 1597–1653. Dutch Admiral who was frequently in battle against **Blake** and was killed in an engagement with **Monck** off the coast of Holland.

TROTSKY, Leon, formerly L D Bronstein 1879–1940. Russian revolutionary and writer. Organised the Red Army but was expelled and assassinated in Mexico. Signature in italic and Russian styles.

TRUDEAU, Pierre Elliott b. 1919. Canadian Liberal statesman. Prime Minister, 1968.

TRUMAN, Harry S 1884–1972. Thirty-third President of the USA.
See also with US Presidents page 205.

TSCHAIKOVSKY (or **TCHAIKOV-SKY**), Piotr Ilych 1840–93. Russian composer. His famous ballets include *Swan Lake* and *Sleeping Beauty*. Variant examples, including one in Russian script.

TUBMAN, William J S 1895–1971. President of Liberia, 1944–71.

TURENNE, Henri de la Tour d'Auvergne, Vicomte de 1611–75. French Marshal. **Napoleon** considered him the greatest of all military commanders.

TURGENEV (or **TOURGUENEFF**), Ivan S 1818–83. Russian novelist. His greatest work was *Fathers and Children*. Variant signatures.

TURGOT, A Robert Jacques 1727–81. French economist and statesman. Comptroller-General of Finance to **Louis XVI**.

TURNER, Joseph Mallord William 1775–1851. English landscape and seascape painter in water-colours.
ALS from Turner, when elderly, to his friend the still young art critic and writer **John Ruskin**. Undated *c.* 1845. A typical example of the added interest of a letter written by one well-known person to another, as discussed in the Introduction. (Author's Collection.)

TUSSAUD, Marie 1760–1850. 'Madame Tussaud'. Swiss modeller in wax. Her life-size collection of historical figures formed the foundation of the permanent exhibition in London.

TWAIN, Mark, pseudonym of Samuel L Clemens 1835–1910. American humorist of *Tom Sawyer* and *Huckleberry Finn* fame. His signature in both forms.

TYLER, John 1790–1862. Tenth President of the USA. Annexed Texas to the Union. Tyler had been Vice-President but when **W H Harrison** died after only one month in office, he succeeded as President. Also see with US Presidents page 204.

UNDSET, Sigrid 1882–1949. Norwegian Nobel Prize-winning (1928) novelist. Her major work was *Kristin Lavransdatter*, a trilogy.

URIS, Leon b. 1924. American novelist. Known in particular for his *Exodus*.

UTRILLO, Maurice 1883–1955. French painter, in particular of Paris street scenes. His painting signature includes a final capital 'V' for the surname of his mother, the painter Suzanne Valadon.

VALENTINO, Rudolph 1895–1926. Italian-born American film actor. The leading screen 'hero' of the silent films, he became a legend in his lifetime and a part of film history.

Cordially yours,
Rudolph Valentino
Strand Theatre,
Aug. 16, 1924.

VALÉRY, Paul (A) 1871–1945. French poet and philosopher.

Paul A. Valéry

VALETTE, Jean Parisot de La 1494–1568. French knight. As Grand Master successfully defended Malta against the Turks in the great siege of 1565. He founded the island's capital, named after him, Valletta.

VANBRUGH, Sir John 1664–1726. English architect and dramatist. As a playwright a master of Restoration comedy. Designed Blenheim Palace for **Marlborough**.
ALS concerning the building of Blenheim Palace, 1707. (The British Library.)

London. Dec: ye 10th 1707

VAN BUREN, Martin 1782–1862. Eighth President of the USA.
Also see with US Presidents page 204.

VANCOUVER, George *c.* 1757–98. English navigator. Explored Australasian and North American Pacific coasts.
Vancouver Island and city named after him.

VANDERBILT, Cornelius II 1843–99. American financier and transport tycoon. His signature should not be confused with that of his father, similarly named, who founded the Vanderbilt 'empire'.

VAN DER POST, Laurens b. 1906. South African writer.
See PS with others page 35 under **Campbell**.

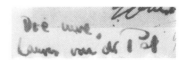

VAN DYCK, Sir Anthony 1599–1641. Flemish painter. A great master of portraiture, he was Court painter to **Charles I** of England.

VAN'T HOFF, Jacobus Hendricus 1852–1911. Dutch Nobel Prize-winning (1901) chemist. The first to apply thermodynamics to chemical reactions. Variant signatures, 1874 and much more flamboyant, 1910.

VAUBAN, Sébastien le Prestre, Marquis de 1633–1707. French military engineer and Marshal. Constructed fortress defences around France.

VAUGHAN WILLIAMS, Ralph 1872–1958. British composer.
Holograph musical extract from his *A Sea Symphony*. (Author's Collection.)

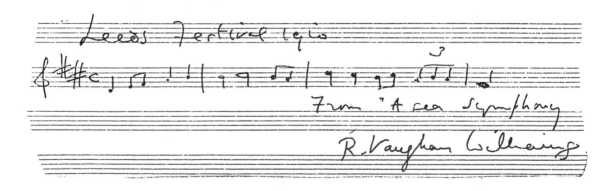

VEGA CARPIO, Lope Félix de 1562–1635. Foremost Spanish dramatist and poet. Credited with at least 1500 plays!

VELASQUEZ, Diego R de Silva y 1599–1660. Spanish painter. Variant painting signatures.

VENIZELOS, Eleutherios K 1864–1936. Six times Prime Minister of Greece.

VERDI, Giuseppe 1813–1901. Italian composer of the operas *La Traviata*, *Aïda*, *Il Trovatore* and *Rigoletto*. Autographically, the most sought-after of the later Italian composers.

VERLAINE, Paul 1844–96. French symbolist and decadent poet.

VERMEER (of Delft) Jan 1632–75. Dutch painter, particularly of interiors. Not to be confused with the two Jan Vermeers of Haarlem.

VERNE, Jules 1828–1905. French novelist. An early pioneer of science fiction in his novels *Twenty Thousand Leagues under the Sea* and *Voyage to the Centre of the Earth*. He also wrote the classic *Around the World in Eighty Days*. ANS on his visiting card. (Author's Collection.)

VERONESE, Paolo, correctly P Caliari or Cagliari 1525–88. Verona-born Italian master painter of the Venetian school. A painting signature as Veronese and his usual signature.

VESPUCCI, Amerigo 1451–1512. Florentine-born Spanish explorer of the coasts of the New World. America named after him.
End portion of an ALS, July 1500 and a signature, December 1508. (Supplied by the Library of the Instituto de Cultura Hispanica, Madrid.)

VICTOR, Claude Perrin, Duc de Belluno 1764–1841. French Marshal.
See also with Napoleonic Marshals page 179.

VICTOR EMMANUEL II, 1820–78. King of Sardinia who became the first King of a unified Italy, 1861–78.

VICTOR EMMANUEL III, 1869–1947. King of Italy 1900–46. Abdicated in favour of his son Umberto.

VICTORIA, 1819–1901. Queen of Great Britain and Ireland. Empress of India.
See also with British Sovereigns page 25.

VIGNY, Alfred (V), Comte de 1797–1863. French man of letters. One of his greatest works was *Chatterton*.

VILLA, Francisco, 'Pancho' 1877–1923. Mexican revolutionary leader. A former bandit, correctly named Doroteo Arango. Assassinated.

VINCENT DE PAUL, Saint 1576–1660. French priest and saint. Founded the Congregation of the Mission and the Sisters of Charity, both called Vincentians. A very rare autograph.

VINCI, Leonardo da 1452–1519. Florentine painter, sculptor, architect, scientist and engineer. One of the most remarkable personalities in the history of man. Painted the celebrated *Mona Lisa* and *The Last Supper*. Studied, and produced annotated drawings thereof, such subjects as hydraulics, meteorology, biology and aeronautics, anticipating, *inter alia*, the inventions, centuries later, of the aeroplane and the submarine.

Examples of his signature and 'mirror-writing' with annotated drawings. (The British Library.)

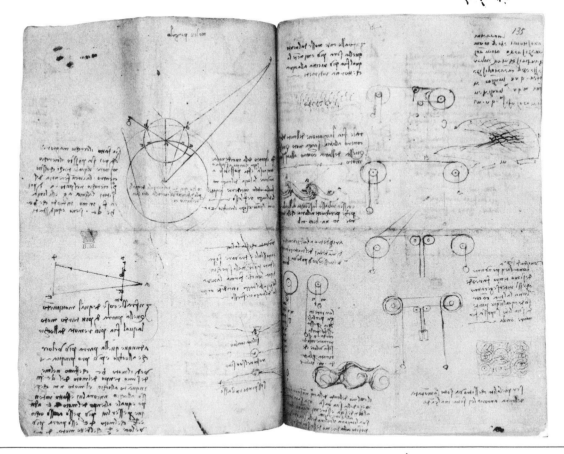

VISHINSKY, or VYSHINSKY Andrei Y 1883–1954. Soviet Foreign Minister 1949–53. Russia's Chief Prosecutor at the Nuremberg Trials.
Also see signature under **Stalin**.

V - W

VIVALDI, Antonio *c*. 1676–1741. Italian composer and violinist.
Autographically rare.

VLAMINCK, Maurice de 1876–1958. French painter, of the Fauvist school.

VOLTA, Count Alessandro 1745–1827. Italian physicist and pioneer in electricity. The unit of electrical force, the volt, named after him.

VOLTAIRE, François M Arouet de 1694–1778. French philosopher, satirist and man of letters.
Autographically much in demand. Care is necessary in identifying Voltaire's autograph as a secretary wrote in a very similar hand.
Variant autographs signed in full. Voltaire also sometimes signed only 'V'.

VON BRAUN, Wernher 1912–77. German-born American rocket expert. Perfected the V2 in World War II. Directed American space-flight projects. This example is probably by autopen.

VORSTER, B Johannes b. 1915. Prime Minister of South Africa, 1966.

WAGNER, Richard 1813–83. German composer and writer. Operas include *Lohengrin*, *Tannhauser* and the four-cycle *Ring of the Nibelung*. He wrote his own librettos.
Variant signatures.

WAGNER-JAUREGG, Julius 1857–1940. Austrian neurologist. Won Nobel Prize, 1927, for his discovery of a treatment for general paralysis by the infection of the subject with malaria.

WALDEGRAVE, James, 2nd Earl 1715–63. English statesman.
See also with British Prime Ministers page 68.

WALLACE, Edgar 1875–1932. Prolific English author of thrillers such as *The Four Just Men* and African adventure stories, including *Sanders of the River*.

WALLENSTEIN, Albrecht E W von, Prince of Sagan and Duke of Friedland 1583–1634. Austrian General in the Thirty Years War.

WALPOLE, Horace, 4th Earl of Orford 1717–97. English man of letters.
Horace was a common name in the Walpole family and collectors must be careful with identification of his autograph.
Two examples are shown, a signature as 'H Walpole' and a part ALS signed 'Orford' after succeeding to the Earldom in 1791, dated from Strawberry Hill, 13 September 1792 to Samuel Lysons on historical and literary matters. (Theo Johnson Collection.)

WALPOLE, Sir Robert, 1st Earl of Orford 1676–1745. Britain's first Prime Minister.
See also with British Prime Ministers page 68.

WALSINGHAM, Sir Francis *c.* 1530–90. English Tudor statesman. Headed **Queen Elizabeth I**'s espionage system. A small faction considers him to be the author of **Shakespeare**'s plays.

WALTER, Bruno 1876–1962. German-Jewish orchestral conductor, who changed his name from Schlesinger.

W

WALTON, Izaak 1593–1683. English writer. His masterpiece is *The Compleat Angler*.
An uncommon autograph.

WALTON, Sir William (T) b. 1902. British composer.

WASHINGTON, Booker T 1856–1915. American Negro educator and reformer.

WASHINGTON, George 1732–99. American statesman and soldier. Victorious commander in the War of Independence and first President of the USA.
A personally signed ticket in the Mountain Road Lottery of 1768, slightly damaged. (Author's Collection.)
Also an LS to his 'Great and Good Friend', the King of England concerning the exchange of ratifications of a treaty of amity, commerce and navigation. Signed by Washington at Philadelphia, 25 August 1795. (Public Record Office, London.) Also see with US Presidents, page 204.

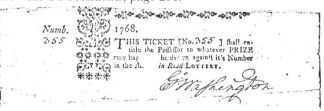

WASSERMANN, Jakob 1873–1934. German novelist.
A typical example of his miniscule autograph.

WATSON-WATT, Sir Robert 1892–1973. British physicist. Pioneered development of radar.

WATT, James 1736–1819. Scottish engineer and inventor. Pioneer of the steam engine. The power unit 'watt' named after him. Care must be taken not to confuse his autograph with that of his son.

WATTEAU, (J) Antoine 1684–1721. French painter, particularly of pastoral subjects.
An example of one of his methods of signing his pictures.

WATTS, Isaac 1674–1748. English theologian and hymnist. Wrote, amongst some 600 hymns, 'O God our help in ages past'.

WAUGH, Evelyn (A St J) 1903–66. English novelist.

WAYNE, John. Colourful American film actor. Hero of many Western epics.

WEBB, Matthew 1848–83. Captain Webb, English swimmer. The first person to swim the English Channel. Drowned trying to swim across Niagara rapids.

WEBER, Carl Maria (F E) von 1786–1826. German composer. A scarce autograph. Important ALS in English sending the score of the First Act of his opera *Oberon* to Sir George Smart, at whose house he died less than three months later. Dated 16 March 1826. (Author's Collection.)

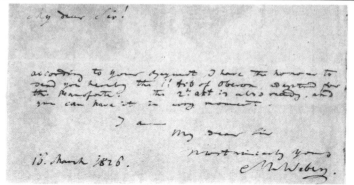

WEBSTER, Daniel 1782–1852. American statesman. Secretary of State under Presidents **W H Harrison**, **Tyler** and **Fillmore**.

WEDGWOOD, Josiah 1730–95. English potter. Originated Wedgwood Ware. **John Flaxman** was responsible for some of the designs produced at his works at Etruria.

WEISSMULLER, Johnny b. 1904. American swimmer and film actor. Established 67 world swimming records and won five Olympic gold medals. Portrayed 'Tarzan' in nineteen films.

WEIZMANN, Chaim 1874–1952. Zionist leader. Founder and first President of Israel. Distinguished chemist and scholar.

WELLES, (G) Orson b. 1915. American film actor and director. Responsible for writing, directing, producing and acting in the film classic *Citizen Kane*.

WELLINGTON, Arthur Wellesley, Duke of 1769–1852. English soldier and statesman. The victor of Waterloo and the Peninsular Campaign.

Autographers must be careful not to confuse his holograph with that of one of his secretaries which is very similar. This example is from a letter to Sir **Thomas Lawrence** at the British Museum. Also see signature with British Prime Ministers page 68.

WELLS, H(erbert) G(eorge) 1866–1946. English man of letters.

WESLEY, Charles 1707–88. English hymnist. Joined with his brother in the founding of the Methodist Church.

WESLEY, John 1703–91. English theologian and evangelist. The founder of Methodism.

One of very few divines whose autograph is greatly sought after.

WEST, Benjamin 1738–1820. American painter who became President of the British Royal Academy.

Autograph admission card to the Royal Academy, 28 March 1815. (Author's Collection.)

WEST, Mae b. 1892. American film actress. Famed for her tongue-in-cheek invitation, 'Come up and see me sometime!'

WHISTLER, James A M 1834–1903. American artist who lived largely in London.
Holograph invitation signed with his butterfly signature. (Author's Collection.)

WHITGIFT, John *c.* 1530–1604. English churchman. Responsible for 94 theological works.
Signature as Archbishop of Canterbury – 'Cantuar', latinised form.

WHITMAN, Walt(er) 1819–92. American poet. The author of *Leaves of Grass*, he spent some years as a lowly civil servant.

WHITNEY, Eli 1765–1825. American inventor of the cotton gin, etc.

WHITTIER, John Greenleaf 1807–92. American poet and abolitionist.
Whittier's signature changed a lot. Two variant examples are shown.

WHITTLE, Sir Frank 1907–75. English aeronautical engineer. Developed the jet engine.

WILBERFORCE, William 1759–1833. British reformer. The leading slave-trade abolitionist.

WILDE, Oscar (F O'F W) 1854–1900. Irish poet and dramatist. Author of *Lady Windermere's Fan*, *The Importance of Being Earnest* and *Dorian Grey*.
An important literary autograph.
ALS to a lady regarding a literary contribution to the magazine *Woman's World*. (Author's Collection.)

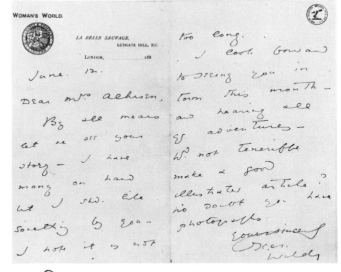

WILDER, Thornton (N) 1897–1975. American novelist and playwright. Won the Pulitzer Prize with his *The Bridge of San Luis Rey*.

WILLIAM I, 1027–87. 'William the Conqueror'. Duke of Normandy and first Norman King of England 1066–87.
An excessively rare attested *signum* on a document also signed by Queen Matilda and others. A grant of church land undated but *c*. 1070. (The British Library.)

WILLIAM III, 1650–1702. William of Orange. King of Great Britain and Ireland 1689–1702.
See also with British Sovereigns page 25.

WILLIAM IV, 1765–1837. King of Great Britain and Ireland 1830–7.
See also with British Sovereigns page 25.

WILLIAM (WILHELM) I, 1797–1888. King of Prussia from 1861–and first Emperor of Germany from 1871.

WILLIAM (WILHELM) II, 1859–1941. Emperor of Germany 1888–1918. 'The Kaiser' whose ambitions foundered with defeat in World War I.

WILLIAM (I) THE SILENT, 1533–84. Prince of Orange. The first Stadtholder of the Dutch Republic which he led in its struggle for independence from Spain.
Variant autographs as Guill(aum)e de Nassau, 1555 and to his mother as Prince of Orange, 1580.

WILLIAM OF WYKEHAM 1324–1404. English bishop, Lord Chancellor and educationalist. Founded Winchester College. A rare autograph.

WILLIAMS, Tennessee, pseudonym of Thomas L Williams, b. 1911. American dramatist. Plays include *A Streetcar Named Desire* and *Cat on a Hot Tin Roof*.

WILLS-MOODY, now Roark, Helen b. 1905. American tennis player who won a record eight Wimbledon Ladies Singles Championships between 1927 and 1938.

WILSON, Sir (James) Harold b. 1916. British Labour statesman. Three times Prime Minister.
See also with British Prime Ministers page 69.

WILSON, (Thomas) Woodrow 1856–1924. Twenty-eighth President of the USA. Brought America into World War I. Nobel Peace Prize-winner, 1919. See also with US Presidents page 205.

WODEHOUSE, Sir P(elham) G(renville) 1881–1975. English-born American-naturalised humorist. Created Jeeves and Bertie Wooster.

WOFFINGTON, Margaret ('Peg') 1720–60. Irish actress. Greatly admired by **Garrick**.
An uncommon and historic theatrical autograph.

WOLFE, James 1727–59. British General. The captor of Quebec, where he was killed. A rare autograph.

WOLSEY, Thomas c. 1475–1530. English Cardinal and Lord Chancellor under **Henry VIII**.
Signature as Cardinal and Archbishop of York ('Ebor', latinised form).
Also a Privy Council Warrant for the delivery of £2000 to the Merchants of the Staple at Calais. With this they are to buy two very different articles of merchandise, 'artillery habilments of Warre' and wine for the King. (**Henry VIII**). Wolsey's signature 'Thomas Wulcy' is the last of the five Councillors who have signed. His rival Thomas Howard, Duke of Norfolk the victim of Flodden Field is the first and the others are Richard Foxe, Bishop of Winester, Charles Somerset, Earl of Worcester and Sir Thomas Lovell. Receipted by the Merchants below. Dated 25 November 1513. (Author's Collection.)

WOOD, Haydn 1882–1959. English composer. Holograph musical extract from his popular ballad 'Roses of Picardy'. (Author's Collection.)

Roses are shining in Picardy to the

Haydn Wood

WOOLF, Virginia (A) 1882–1941. English novelist and essayist.
A sought-after literary autograph.

is a railway line direct from Richmond; I could find you a train.

Yours Virginia Woolf.

WORDSWORTH, William 1770–1850. English Poet Laureate.
A major poetical autograph though not yet scarce. Variant signatures.

Wm Wordsworth

W Wordsworth

WOUK, Herman b. 1915. American novelist. Author of *The Caine Mutiny*.

Herman Wouk

WREN, Sir Christopher 1632–1723. English architect, particularly of St Paul's Cathedral and other London churches.

April 23. 1692

Sr this poor Child Robert Little (whose honest Father dyed very poor in the Kings service of the Workes) is the Orphan I had hopes might have been received into Christchurch Hospitall, and I was lately told by Mr Treasurer that the Govern.do haue referred the mater to Yr Wp. and not doubting of your Charity, of which I knowe the Child to be a fit Object: I take the confidence to request Your assistance that he may be admitted, which I shall allwaies acknowledge as a particular favour to

Sr
Your most humble servant
Chr Wren

WRIGHT, Orville 1871–1948, and his elder brother Wilbur, 1867–1912. American pioneer aviators who made the first ever power-driven aeroplane flight, travelling 852 ft in 59 sec, 17 December 1903.

Orville Wright.

Wilbur Wright.

WYSZYNSKI, Stepan b. 1901. Polish Cardinal-Archbishop of Warsaw who suffered imprisonment for resistance to Communism.

Błogosławi
Stefan Kard. Wyszył.

YEATS, William Butler 1865–1939. Irish poet and dramatist. Won Nobel Prize, 1923. A sought-after literary autograph.

YOUNG, Brigham 1801–77. American Mormon leader. First Governor of Utah and founder of Salt Lake City.

YPSILANTI, Alexander 1792–1828 and Demetrios 1793–1832. Greek patriot brothers who struggled for the independence of their country from Turkey.

ZAHAROFF, Sir Basil 1850–1936. Anglo-Greek financier, arms manufacturer and philanthropist.

ZAHIR SHAH, Mohammed b. 1914. King of Afghanistan from 1933 to 1973, when he was overthrown.

ZAIMIS, Alexander 1855–1936. Greek statesman. Six times Prime Minister of Greece and President 1929–35.

ZATOPEK, Emil b. 1922. Czech athlete. One of the greatest long-distance runners of all time, he broke thirteen world records and won four Olympic Gold Medals, three in 1952 and one in 1956.

ZEPPELIN, Ferdinand, Count von 1838–1917. German soldier and aeronaut. Designed and built the first rigid-type airship, the *Graf Zeppelin* named after him. Zeppelin's autograph is in demand as pioneers of aviation form a specialised autographic field.
PS. (Author's Collection.)

ZOG I, Ahmed Bey Zogu 1895–1961. King of Albania 1928–46. Formerly Prime Minister and President.

ZOLA, Emile 1840–1902. French novelist and man of letters. Championed the cause of the wrongfully imprisoned **Dreyfus**.

ZWEIG, Stefan 1881–1942. Austrian-born British naturalised Jewish writer. Biographer of **Balzac** and **Dickens** and translator of **Ben Jonson**.

ZWINGLI, Huldreich 1484–1531. Swiss Protestant reformer, humanist and religious leader.
A portion of an ALS beginning with his name. This is written in the same way as he signed his signature. A scarce and important Swiss autograph.

ZWORYKIN, Vladimir Kosma b. 1889. Russian-born American naturalised physicist. A pioneer of television and of the electron microscope, he invented the iconoscope.